LAMBS
AMONG
WOLVES

Foreword by Michael W. Smith

LAMBS
AMONG
WOLVES

BOB BRINER
Author of *Roaring Lambs*

ZondervanPublishingHouse
Grand Rapids, Michigan

A Division of HarperCollinsPublishers

Lambs Among Wolves
Copyright © 1995 by Robert A. Briner

Requests for information should be addressed to:

▥ ZondervanPublishingHouse
Grand Rapids, Michigan 49530

Library of Congress Cataloging-in-Publication Data

Briner, Bob.
    Lambs among wolves : how christians are influencing american culture /
Bob Briner.
        p   cm.
    ISBN: 0-310-48810-9 (hardcover)
        1. Christianity and the arts—United States. 2. Christianity and cul-
ture. 3. Church and the world. 4. Christian biography—United States. 5.
Evangelicalism—United States. 6. United States—Moral conditions. 7.
United States—Church history—20th century. 8. United States—Social con-
ditions—1980–   I. Title.
BR115.A8B75   1995
261.5'7-dc 20
                                                                    95-30467
                                                                    CIP

International/Trade Paper Edition 0-310-48819-2

This edition printed on acid-free paper and meets the American National
Standards Institute Z39.48 standard.

Edited by Jan Ortiz

Printed in the United States of America

Published in association with Sealy M. Yates, Literary Agent

95 96 97 98 99 00 01 02 /❖ DH/ 10 9 8 7 6 5 4 3 2 1

For our son, Rob,
who has taught us so much.

✺

Contents

Foreword

The first time I opened the book *Roaring Lambs* by Bob Briner, I could not put it down. I was amazed that this man had captured in a book the philosophy behind what I and a handful of other recording artists had been trying to do for so long with our music. I had never thought of myself as a "roaring lamb" before, but after reading Bob's book, I realized that he articulated exactly what I hoped to do with my music. I wanted to be salt and light in a world of darkness, and for my light to truly shine, I knew I had to go before a wider audience than the Christians who had supported my music so faithfully in the past. They were a faithful flock, but I could not help but remember the parable of the lost sheep, the one that the Good Shepherd left the flock to find.

Roaring Lambs taught that Christians could (and should) "roar" in the arts by writing books, songs, and screenplays that accurately portray the life-changing message of hope found in the Gospel. Why have Christian songs, movies, and books had so little impact in the real world up to this point? Perhaps it is because we have whispered rather than roared. It is up to us to take our message to the world, but to get the world's ear, our creative works of art and our ability to perform them have to be on the same professional level as anything the world has to offer. God wants us to offer our best to him. Bob's book has energized many of us to be bolder in the face of the "lions" who often seem ready to tear us to bits. Sadly, many of these lions come from our own ranks ... people who do not understand what we are trying to do.

Suddenly, *Roaring Lambs*, with no hype, was all the buzz in Nashville. It was not really aimed at the Christian music community; Bob is a sports and television executive. Just the same, it gave many of us our marching orders and voiced desires that had simmered under the surface for a long time in the hearts of many. Whether we are reaching a broader audience with our music or writing and singing Christian music in churches and colleges, it is all-important to be roaring lambs because all of us are called to roar. We have all needed to put into action the message of *Roaring Lambs*.

Recognizing that God has given me the gift of music means that I have to use this gift for his glory. For me, that means writing some songs for the church and some songs for the world that is beyond the smaller, evangelical Christian circle. Critics call this "crossing over" and "selling out," but for me that does not matter; because I know that I am doing what God has called me to do—make a positive difference in the lives of people who, in turn, can change the world.

In my opinion, that is what Bob Briner did with *Roaring Lambs*. His follow-up book, *Lambs Among Wolves,* is sure to do the same, as it reminds us that we are not being sent into a world that will always embrace our message. As we take our creative endeavors and talents to the masses, we have to be prepared to face some hostility. Some radio stations will not play our music; some studios will not turn our screenplays into films. But that does not take away our calling. If we do not go, who will?

Roaring Lambs laid the foundation and now *Lambs Among Wolves* builds on Bob's theme of Christians who are salt and light through the performing arts. Bob shows how this philosophy is being played out in the lives of real people. Some of these people are instantly recognizable. Others are not. Whether they are well-known or not, they all share a common denominator. They come from many different fields and many different places, but they are Christians making a difference in the world around them. They are lambs among wolves. I am humbled that Bob has included my story in this book.

Bob and I hope that *Lambs Among Wolves* will inspire you to make a difference in your world. Our prayer is that this book will be a driving force to move Christians out into the world where they are so desperately needed. It is in the darkness that light shines the brightest. Let your light shine. You can change your world.

Michael W. Smith

Acknowledgments

More than ever, I know that a book is a team effort. Someone may have his name prominently displayed on the dust jacket, but he is only representing his team. I am so fortunate that the team that brought *Roaring Lambs* and *Squeeze Play* to fruition was also intact for *Lambs Among Wolves* and that we were also able to add another star-quality player.

First of all, I want to pay special tribute to my "designated hitters" from Zondervan. Publisher Scott Bolinder and senior acquisitions editor Lyn Cryderman, at various times and in various ways, made the book happen. They generated the idea for this book. When barriers arose, they knocked them down with whatever force was necessary. When I was the barrier, they whipped me into shape. Scott, Lyn, thanks for staying on the team.

My friends at Zondervan were aided and abetted by superagent Sealy Yates. He too was instrumental in the birth of *Lambs Among Wolves* and is one of the great utility players in Christian publishing—going into the game whenever there is a need. Thanks, Sealy.

As always, Dr. Ray Pritchard, the senior pastor at Calvary Memorial Church in Oak Park, Illinois, provided scriptural and theological insights and direction for me. Any deviations from the straight and narrow are mine, not his. I appreciate you, Pastor Ray.

Mary Ann Van Meter, my longtime secretary-assistant at Pro-Serv Television, was on the team for the first two books and played an even bigger role in the typing and production of *Lambs Among Wolves*. She is a great team player and has my gratitude.

My wife Marty read the material as it was being written and provided invaluable advice and suggestions. She is one of God's greatest gifts to me.

Those listed above constitute a strong lineup. With Zondervan's help, we were also able to sign our number-one draft choice. Readers of Christian publications are familiar with Joe Maxwell's byline; he is a star. Joe contributed immeasurably to *Lambs Among Wolves* by doing much of the research, conducting many of the interviews, and providing insights and direction for the entire book. He is an MVP.

I am most grateful to my friend, Michael W. Smith, for his wonderful foreword. His is only the most visible of the efforts of my friends in Christian music who have contributed to this book—including Barry Landis, Chaz Corzine, Michelle Fink, Lesley Burbridge, Neal Joseph, John Styll, Pastor Scott Patty, Pastor Scotty Smith, Dick Tunney, and Charlie Peacock. My thanks to each of them.

Finally, my most important thanks goes to the tremendously inspirational lambs who are out there among the wolves, bringing the salt and light of the Shepherd to a world in desperate need.

Preface

Each roaring lamb is unique. Each is special. Certainly each who seeks to be obedient to Jesus' call to be salt in the world has his or her own way of fulfilling that call. The NFL quarterback who chose to recite the lyrics of "In Christ Alone" on national television certainly has a different approach to being salt than does the man in rural Illinois who quietly restores neglected cemeteries as a means of witnessing to those whose loved ones are buried there. Both approaches are valid and valued. There is no template, no cookie cutter, when it comes to roaring lambs, when it comes to being salt. Christ asks each of us to begin where we are with what we have.

Even with all the uniqueness in approach and methods, there still seems to be common threads running through the lives of those who are most successful at roaring, at being salt, at being obedient. As you meet these people, you will note these common threads. It will be profitable to take a close look at the consistent features of their lives in these early pages, since we will focus on the ways in which roaring lambs are the same in order to learn from them.

Unfortunately, it seems that the most common thread running through the lives of those who most diligently seek to impact the culture for Christ is the certainty that they will be criticized. We expect those who do not know Jesus to criticize those who seek to represent him. Salt bites and stings as it penetrates, cleanses, and preserves. A clear, uncluttered, undiluted representation of Jesus almost always makes people uncomfortable. Criticism follows. However, roaring lambs almost always draw criticism from within the church, from fellow Christians, as well. Many do not understand a roaring lamb's in-depth involvement with the world as he or she attempts to be the salt they are admonished to be. Many will criticize these lambs' close association with non-Christians and their involvement in so-called secular activities. Expect this kind of criticism. It goes with the territory. It happened to me when I left my coaching job on a Christian college campus to take a job with pro football's Miami Dolphins. There is a strong possibility that you will also be a target when you move boldly into your world with the salt of the Gospel. Do not seek criticism. Do not treat it cavalierly. Examine it in the light of Scripture. Use it to sharpen your focus and to keep your motives and life pure. See it as an iron-sharpening tool. Do not be bitter toward those who criticize. Be patient with them. Take the time to explain to them the concept of being salt, and then move on. Do not let criticism, or reacting to it, tie you down. Do not let it deter you. Expect it. Be obedient. Be salt. Be a roaring lamb.

Another of the most common threads running through the lives of the roaring lambs whom I know, the ones you will meet in the following pages, is that they had to pay their dues. They have done this by working very hard, sometimes for long periods of time. Certainly, they were attempting to be salt along the way, but they reached their maximum effectiveness after considerable effort. Being the salt that Jesus asks us to be is not an impulse kind of thing; it is a commitment to a way of life. The NFL quarterback who recited the lyrics worked at his trade for many years, took many hits, was sacked many times, and suffered many interceptions before he earned the right to stand up for Jesus before a national television audience. To be at the right place at the right time calls for diligence and determination—over time.

Now, it is very important to know that being in the right place, at the right time, does *not* mean to wait for a special moment, the perfect circumstances, to begin. It most definitely does not mean that. Before that wonderful moment on NBC, that quarterback had been quietly and effectively representing Jesus and his cause for many years. Christ wants us to begin where we are with what we have and to continue to earn the hearing we will eventually have.

The roaring lambs that God has allowed me to know have not only been willing to go the distance, to hang in there for the long haul, they also have had an unwavering single-minded commitment to excellence. They might not articulate this even in their own minds, but their lives seem to say, "How can I represent the excellence of the Savior, if I am not willing to be the very best I can be?" Jesus does not ask us to be more than we can be. He does not expect me to sing like Michael W. Smith, teach like Chuck Swindoll, or write like Philip Yancey. He does expect me to do what I do as unto him, which means doing it the best way I know how. Roaring lambs seem, almost intuitively, to understand this. Those of us who seek to be roaring lambs need to appropriate this trait for our own lives. Make a commitment to excellence.

A corollary to a commitment to excellence is a never-give-up attitude. My friend Joe Maxwell, who has contributed significantly to this book, calls this a "God-guided drive to succeed." As you might expect, those who are most successful at being salt are those who have a God-given goal or vision and refuse to give up seeking it. Eventually, God honors their sanctified tenacity. The apostle Paul wrote about and lived this kind of single-mindedness. Twentieth-century roaring lambs need to do the same.

God has allowed me to meet a young, Christian, would-be screenwriter who lives in Dallas. He has talent, but it is very difficult to break into this demanding, but strategically important profession. He keeps on keeping on and is an inspiration both to me and to many others. His scripts get read in Hollywood, and, even if they never get produced, he has provided a constant stream of salt for those who read his steadily improving screenplays.

People who do *not* know Jesus sometimes have this same willingness to work hard and commitment to excellence. With roaring lambs, the significant difference—the essential added ingredient—is selflessness. They are selfless in their work and aspirations. They are not self-motivated, but God motivated. They are not consumed by a career, but are consumed by God while pursuing a career. You will see this very clearly in the people we profile in the following pages.

Finally, it seems almost axiomatic and obvious to everyone that, to be a real roaring lamb, it is necessary to be able to attract non-Christians rather than attack them. Sadly, this is not apparent to many Christians. Too many feel that the way to righteousness and obedience is through lashing out at the evil that they see about them. The successful and joyful roaring lambs you will meet in this book understand that their call is not to protest but to proclaim. They are to do everything possible to lift the wonderful Savior high up for all to see. Roaring lambs are not out berating non-Christians. They are not bogged down in a series of causes, boycotts, petitions, or protests. They recognize that Christ alone is the one to right the wrongs by changing men and women one heart at a time. They seek to attract non-Christians through lives of excellent, selfless service. This is not some mystical or arcane way of living. Rather, it is living uncommon lives for him in the very common places in which they find themselves. Roaring lambs do this. You can too. Jesus never asks anyone to do the impossible. With him all things are possible as we commit ourselves to his holy cause.

As you read about the servants of God in the following pages, watch for those common threads in their stories. As you begin to roar, see if you do not begin to experience some of the same things in your own life.

Introduction

Some of you may be surprised to know that old guys can still learn. By God's grace, even old Texans can still learn. The interval between *Roaring Lambs* and *Lambs Among Wolves* has been perhaps the most intense and productive time of learning in all my fifty-eight years.

God has seen fit to bring a veritable flood of information rolling over me during the past several months. First of all, I have heard personally and individually from more than three thousand people who have read *Roaring Lambs*. If you have not read *Roaring Lambs*, I encourage you to do so. Although *Lambs Among Wolves* will be meaningful for you even if you have not read the book that spawned it, you will have more of a foundation if you first read *Roaring Lambs*. The people who have written have very kindly and very helpfully shared many of the thoughts, ideas, experiences, and frustrations evoked by their reading my book. I have learned a tremendous amount from their wonderful letters as well as from those who made phone calls.

I have also been speaking to a wide variety of audiences in all parts of the country. Churches, colleges, writers' conferences, men's retreats, ministers' conferences, prayer breakfasts, and professional associations are examples of some of these groups. These appearances have spanned the country from California to New England and from Florida to Michigan. Inevitably, in connection with each of these, I have had the opportunity to have some very meaningful and informative conversations with the people in attendance. They have taught me much more than I have taught them.

As incredible as it seems, I have also appeared on more than one hundred radio and television programs to discuss *Roaring Lambs*. Again, these programs have been broadcast in all parts of the country, in all kinds of locales. From rural farm-belt communities to great metropolitan areas, from Seattle to Key West, people have heard about *Roaring Lambs* from their own radio and television sets. Some of these broadcasts and telecasts have been national, like Pat Robertson's *700 Club*. The most important thing to know about these radio and television appearances is that the vast majority of them were call-in programs. In other words, the listeners and viewers did not just listen to me, they also *talked* to me. They asked questions and gave me their opinions—sometimes very forcefully. Every time I participated, I learned.

So, because I wrote *Roaring Lambs*, because God has been so gracious, and because of the kindness of hundreds of people, I have been very privileged to have a learning experience that is unique, at least unique in my life. In *Lambs Among Wolves*, I want to share with you much of what I learned.

Overall, one of the most important things I learned is how little I knew. Even in the specific areas that I addressed in *Roaring Lambs*, God's people are doing so much more than I knew about or ever imagined. I want to share the new things that I have learned about how wonderful servants of Jesus Christ are being salt and light in very effective, inspiring ways. These range from very high-profile people, whose names you will instantly recognize, to people very few know but who are also experiencing the great joy that comes from obedience, from being actively engaged on the front lines of his great cause.

I have also learned that most Christians, though inspired by the magnificence of Jesus and motivated by thanksgiving for all he has done for them personally, still do not know specifically what to do and *how* to do it. Currently, too many Christians still fall into the role of spectator, supporting only those relatively few Christian professionals who are engaged in the well-defined, specific tasks for people in the church. This robs too many Christians of the joy of obedience and the exhilarating excitement of engaging in the daily struggle to build God's kingdom in a hostile environment. It keeps Christians from the indescribable thrill of working in direct partnership with God's only Son under the direct leadership of his Holy Spirit in the greatest of all possible enterprises.

In *Lambs Among Wolves*, I hope to show, not through theories or generalities, but through very real examples, exactly *how* Christians—Christians from many walks of life—are exercising their spiritual gifts and are being salt in their worlds. I am praying that these examples will show many who really want to serve, who really want to express their love for the Savior in obedience, exactly how they can do it by integrating their faith with all that they do.

Among the other very general things that I have learned during these past months is how startlingly homogenized the church in America is. I can be talking to a Christian from Wyoming or one from New York and though they might sound slightly different, the questions they ask and the gist of what they are expressing about their faith and their life in the church is almost exactly the same. After doing all those radio call-in shows, I can, in advance, predict almost exactly which questions and comments will be phoned in.

Amazingly, *Roaring Lambs* seems to have been read by people from the whole spectrum of the church in America. It has been a blessing to me to hear both from Catholics and Episcopalians and Quakers and Pentecostals as well as from many other denominations along the continuum. Of all the books I have signed, none brought greater joy than the eight sent by the recently retired Episcopal bishop of Cincinnati, who asked that I sign them for members of his family. I have also been blessed by letter and phone calls from a dear Catholic lady in New Orleans, who continues to tell me that my book corresponds exactly with the message her parish priest is promulgating. She wants me to appear on the archdiocese's radio station. I have spoken in Episcopal churches in New England where I anticipated cold formalism and instead found Christians on fire to tell as many people as possible about who Jesus is and why he came. I have spoken to

Presbyterians, Baptists, Methodists, Free Methodists, Nazarenes, and Evangelical Free, as well as to many Bible and nondenominational Christians. Their concerns are remarkably similar.

Most of the sameness that I have experienced in churches across the country and across denominations has been enlightening, encouraging, and energizing. But, and there always seems to be a but, not all the sameness is positive. I have already mentioned that there are still far too many Christian spectators in the churches. There are far too few people who are actively and positively engaged in regular ongoing activities that are fully integrated in their daily lives and that lift high God's Son for all to see. My amateurish nonscientific explanation for a large part of this is that the scriptural doctrine of the spiritual gifts seems to receive far too little emphasis. To put it in a positive way, those churches that *are* taking the doctrine very seriously, in almost a curricular way, have people among their membership who have identified their spiritual gift or gifts and are exercising them in fruitful, productive ways. Working effectively in the particular area of their spiritual giftedness and experiencing the joy that comes from obedience gives these people a powerful impetus to then begin to fulfill the universal command to be salt and light.

Those people who have *not* been shown how to discover and exercise their spiritual gifts have fallen into the trap of using their pent-up energies for many causes that are "good," but that do not fulfill the very specific demands that Christ makes of his followers. The reality is that if we are fulfilling the Great Commission, exercising our spiritual gift or gifts, and being salt and light, all the other good causes fade into relative insignificance and take their proper place in our lives.

I have been impressed and thrilled to see some churches take the doctrine of spiritual gifts so seriously that they ask their members to take a formal and specific spiritual gift inventory. (Christian publishing companies have these printed inventories available for churches.) Whether with a printed form or through some other method, you and your church should first be discovering the spiritual gifts each person has and then regularly and systematically encouraging them to exercise them. If you cannot generate any enthusiasm for this kind of effort in your church, do not let this rob you of the joy of obedience. Do your own personal inventory. Be sure that you discover your own spiritual gift. *Every Christian has at least one.* Some Christians have several. Look in the books of Romans and Timothy not only to see the list of the gifts but also to understand the simple and very straightforward doctrine related to them.

God has not seen fit to make me a very gifted person, but like every Christian, I do have one spiritual gift. He has seen fit to prosper me to some extent in the sports and television business, enabling me to exercise my gift of giving, or charity. With my wife's help, I try hard to give to people and to causes in a way that will most effectively build his kingdom. My wife has the gift of helps. She is constantly taking food to the ill people of the church, or seeing that prospective brides and prospective mothers in the church have showers so that they are equipped materially for the life ahead. What is your spiritual gift? Is it teaching, administration, helps, giving, evangelism, or one of the others? Discover it. Exercise it. Then move on to becoming effective for him in being salt and light.

Throughout the remainder of this book, we will take a look at many individual Christians who are wonderfully exercising their spiritual gifts and who are also effectively being roaring lambs, bringing the stinging, cleansing, and preserving salt of the Gospel to their areas of influence. Their examples have already been a great inspiration and motivation for me. I trust they will be the same for you.

1

Lambs and the Visual Arts:
Brilliant Forms, Spectacular Colors

In the introduction, I referred to how much I had learned since I wrote *Roaring Lambs*. In no area have I learned more than in the area of the visual arts. There are at least two reasons for this: First, I had much more to learn in this area than in any of the other areas. Second, some of God's choicest people have been willing to tolerate my ignorance and naïveté and have been willing to teach me. The fact that they have not become discouraged but continue to teach me earns my everlasting gratitude.

I extend particular gratitude to Charlie Peacock, the brilliant gospel-music composer, performer, and record producer. Charlie has thought deeply and prayed earnestly about what it means to be a creative Christian. His Ligonier Ministries tape is one of the most cogent discourses I have heard on the subject. The time Charlie has spent with me is greatly appreciated, as are the materials from his Art House ministry. As this is being written, Charlie is working on a book that outlines a scripturally based philosophy of creativity and what it means, or should mean, in the life of a Christian. Watch for this book. I predict that it will be the definitive work in this whole area.

Bill Bippus

In *Roaring Lambs*, I was particularly critical of the visual arts departments of Christian colleges. I wrote, "I would say that at most Christian colleges, art is a sort of academic afterthought. Not much time, attention, or money are devoted to it. The department is usually tucked away in an abandoned building where the students and faculty are ignored. No one is articulating very clearly, or at least very loudly, how the fine-arts program fits into the overall educational and spiritual goals of the Christian college. The results—the paintings and sculpture—for the most part, reflect this neglect" (148–49).

Thanks to the very generous efforts of Professor Bill Bippus of Spring Arbor College in Spring Arbor, Michigan, I now know of at least one Christian college where the visual arts are not an academic afterthought. I am sure there must be others. I hope all of them continue to improve. They need to be sending out more and more graduates who have talent, confidence, and firm biblical underpinnings for a *ministry* in art.

If you ever have the opportunity, visit Spring Arbor College. You will find the art department housed in one of the most prominent, beautiful, and functional buildings on its campus. A classy gallery displaying the work of current and past students occupies the front portion of this spacious facility that also includes studios, workrooms, classrooms, and faculty offices. Even more impressive than the physical plant is the sense of mission articulated by Professor Bippus. He and his colleagues have built the art curriculum on a firm foundation of biblical truth. I want to thank Professor Bippus for the time he has taken to help me understand what art can be in the lives of students, faculty, and alumni in the context of a well-thought-out, Christ-centered college program.

Bill Herring

Some *Roaring Lambs* readers have expressed amazement that I was so interested in meeting David Puttnam, the producer of the movie *Chariots of Fire*, that I got on a plane and flew to London to find him. When you meet Bill Herring, I think you will understand why I would have gone at least as far to see *him*. As it turned out, I did not have to fly anywhere, but I did have to take an automobile trip of almost two thousand miles to the farthest reaches of west Texas. It is among the most worthwhile distances I have ever traveled.

Nationally recognized artist and art philosopher Bill Herring waits for the "golden hour." Strewn across the arid countryside around Bill's west Texas home are bunches of seemingly worthless plants. The scrubby bushes are blue-green teal with half-inch-thick stems rising about three feet out of the sandy soil. Most months the bushes look drab and ordinary. But in early fall, something happens! Atop the bushes, magnificent yellow flowers bloom. The otherwise barren landscape is covered with them. "And the golden hour," explains Bill, a former rancher who has spent days feeding his artistic soul by wandering through living Southwestern landscapes, "is what happens an hour before sunset when light is dancing or skipping across the land from what artists call sidelight. When that light flits across the landscape, it turns everything golden. That's what makes Santa Fe and Taos so magnificent, the light and the particular bush they have there."

A lifetime Texan, this five-foot-ten-inch, 210-pound former rancher wears a star Stetson and blue jeans like he was born in them. In fact, he practically was. When I first met him in a small roadside Tex-Mex eatery, where the enchiladas were as good as they come, Bill was indistinguishable in appearance from the other cowhands and ranchers shoveling in their noontime fix of fiery food. His voice has a range rider's edge. He is a painter, a thinker, and one of the most unique Christians in God's American gallery. The prestigious journal *Southwest Art* says that Bill is "as bold with ideas as he is with his palette," and he swirls the bright, fantastic colors in a constant expressionistic flow onto his canvas. He draws inspiration from the vast landscapes that surround his home near Clint, Texas, where his land runs along the Rio Grande. His conservative roots have sprouted there alongside an independent nature as full of fire as the chilies that grow every season in nearby fields.

Bill's color-splashed Southwestern paintings hang in America's most prestigious galleries as well as in many private collections including those of Ronald Reagan, Peter Coors, and scores of top corporations. His pastels and watercolors have won numerous awards, and he is recognized in *Who's Who in American Art*. A few years ago, Bill was elected president of one of America's oldest and most prestigious art societies, the East Coast-based Knickerbocker Artists. Just recently, he made the short list to fill the presidential vacancy of the National Endowment for the Arts—despite the fact that he once thought the NEA might best be dismantled.

As an artist and a Christian, Bill stands with beauty. That is why he wishes for a golden hour in America, when heretofore scrubby, drab Christians sprout glorious blossoms and beautify an otherwise barren landscape. If they ever do, Bill is sure that God will throw his light on them. The net effect will surely be awesome. It will be beautiful. And beauty, Bill believes, is God's call to humanity—especially Christians. Bill believes, as did Ralph Waldo Emerson, that "beauty is its own reason for existence."

Bill says that Christianity is "more an issue of attraction than it is of promotion"—think about that. It is something all of us need to ponder. And he believes that nothing attracts people more than sheer beauty. "There's this thing going around in Christian circles that a Christian exists to be a channel for God to speak to the world—I do not believe that for one minute. What I believe is this: God created us for beauty—to be beautiful and to enjoy beauty. To the degree that we passionately engage ourselves in this love affair with the Lover of our souls, we will not be able to hide beauty if we try. It is like rabies: the number-one way of getting that disease is to get bit by something that has it. Once you have it, it overwhelms your life."

Bill should know. His father was a full-time rancher and part-time artist; his mother is an artist; his sister is an artist. He grew up getting bit by rabid animals (cows mostly) and beauty. He grew up wanting to "paint on the side for the sheer pleasure of it" and ranch for a living—something he, in fact, did very well for several years. But then things took a turn. His father, in 1982, was ready to sell their ranch, and Bill put together a group of investors to buy it. However, his investors backed out.

Bill, who had graduated from Texas A & M in 1971, began working on a contract basis for other large cattle operations and developed a reputation for working financial wonders with struggling enterprises. Yet he remained frustrated in efforts at landing his own herd, and one day while driving away from a failed deal, he looked through the windshield into the sky. "You know, Lord," he acknowledged, "I think my greatest fear is happening to me." That fear? It was that God would call him to be a painter. Nevertheless, at that moment, Bill already had a clear sense of calling.

"If I moved into the art world, I knew that I had to take all the licks that other artists had to take; or else they would never listen to me. No matter what I was given, I had to suffer. I knew that. I also knew that you can never get artists to listen to you because of their huge egos and megalomaniacal mind-sets. You can't get them to pay any attention to you unless you win them by your work. I was familiar with what Solomon says in Proverbs 18:16: 'A gift opens the way for the giver and ushers him into the presence of the great.' And he says in Proverbs 22:29: 'Do you see a man skilled in his work? He will serve before kings. He will not serve before obscure men!' I knew then to my horror that God had manipulated all of my circumstances in order to send me to this field of men."

Bill had been greatly influenced by Malcolm Muggeridge's *The Third Testament*, in which the now-deceased British journalist and Christian argued that to the degree that Christians overtly identify with Christendom, they will be overtly disregarded by non-Christians.

"Muggeridge makes a case that, over time, Christianity, in many ways and many places, has moved far away from the truth. He often places in these societies people such as Saint Augustine, individuals that he calls 'God's spies,' who are not identified with Christendom and who in the end keep it straight. Good examples are authors Tolstoy and Dostoyevsky. When Lenin and Stalin began to annihilate the existence of the Bible in the Soviet Union, it never occurred to them to eliminate the works of Tolstoy and Dostoyevsky, who were placed as God's spies in that society. By reason of their art, they had been recognized by non-Christians. They were not recognized as Christians but rather were recognized by reason of what they did. So, Stalin never suspected that the works of Dostoyevsky would in any way sustain Christians in that society. The same thing happened with Dietrich Bonhoeffer in Germany. He had to separate from Christendom in order to be a Christian in the context of the Nazi regime. What these examples told me was that I had better do something similar."

Bill also drew inspiration from an old Navigator friend who, along with his wife, came to Texas to visit Bill's family on the way back to their South American mission field. Bill could not help noticing that his friend wore his wedding band on his right hand, not his left.

His friend explained: In the country where they ministered, Catholics wear their wedding bands on their right hand, Protestants on their left. "When we wear a wedding ring on the left hand," his friend continued, "it automatically excludes us from all the social circles of the Catholics. But I believe that God is sending us to this country to reach the Catholics, not the Protestants. But what is really troubling is that if I wear my wedding ring on my right hand, that is a sign to the Protestants that we are not willing to openly identify with Christ, that we are somehow ashamed of him. We are therefore excluded from the social circles of the Protestants, which means for all intents and purposes that we are now excluded from society."

Bill saw the application and implications of his friend's story in his own life. Their observations about cross-cultural ministry, combined with Muggeridge's analysis, convinced him: "I felt that God was now sending me as an ambassador into the art world. I decided to go underground. I did things to separate myself from the local Christian community, which in any circumstance would be viewed as radical. If I was going to relate to the artists in my community, I could not afford to be called a Baptist. I had to literally do what the stay-behind agents did in World War II. Say you were a Frenchman living in German-occupied France, and you were a member of the underground. The last thing you would do is put a little sign on your shirt that said, UNDERGROUND! What you do is you take on the look of the society around you. You become a subservient, docile 'friend' of the Nazis. And by reason of your cooperation, you move into positions of influence and power so that when D-Day comes, they give you a call, and you turn around and use your power or influence to reconquer the land for the French. When I said I had to go underground, I meant that. So I did some very radical things to get Christians to leave me alone because they didn't understand."

Bill repeatedly parked his car out in front of local bars so that Baptists would drive by and think that he had gone astray. He passed Christian friends on the interstate doing ninety miles an hour. Christians began to distance themselves from him. "I broke all of my relationships with the exception of a few, very few, like four individuals, that were also in the world in their professions and who understood what I was doing. I've always felt that I could break from the church as an institution and never lose anything. But I couldn't break from fellowship. If I broke from fellowship, I'd be in serious trouble. So I became, in the classic sense, quite radical. And once I had accomplished that, I began to work on making sure that I could play with the big boys because the big boys were the ones that I felt God wanted me to communicate with."

For the next three years Bill poured himself, along with his and a lot of others' money, into his art. He started paying his dues. "I had to lose a lot of money to understand what the name of the game was. In spite of my business background, I made $29,000 in income and had $32,000 in expenses in my first year as an artist. The next year I had $33,000 in income and $37,000 in expenses. The next year I had $36,000 in income and $42,000 in expenses."

Bill finally found a group of private investors who for three years sent him to "the beautiful places in the world" to paint, and who freed him up financially to be able to compete in major art competitions, where his work gained immediate recognition. In a matter of a few years during the 1980s, his Southwestern paintings were being shown in some of the world's great art galleries. About the same time, Bill was asked to join the prestigious Knickerbocker Artists society; shortly thereafter, the group asked him to join their board and oversee their finances, after having noticed his background in business. It was not too long until they asked Bill to become the society's first non-East Coast president. They wanted Bill to help retool the society to be less Eastern inbred, which he immediately began to do. "I sat back and marveled and couldn't believe that God had opened that avenue," he recalls. Bill was beginning to see the fruits of his underground efforts.

"When you meet an artist," he notes, "the odds of that artist being conservative by nature are slim to none. You just don't find a conservative artist. And you sure don't find an artist who is a Christian. It just does not happen. And so, because it never happens, I was able in this underground context, through the way God does things, to move into these positions because nobody checked me out. They assumed that I was like everybody else and really didn't do their homework."

He laughs about it now. With time, people certainly gained an understanding of where Bill stood on issues of art and life, but by that point, his reputation as an artist and leader in the art world was firmly grounded.

Then came the big shocker. When Bill Clinton became president of the United States, the presidency of the NEA opened. Some Knickerbocker artists—one Virginia man in particular—pushed Bill to consider seeking the position—one of the most influential spots in American art.

"I looked at him and said, 'There's no way. First of all, I've said enough just in what I've published for them to go back and trace my political views. I'm certainly registered as a Republican.' I looked at this guy, and I'd done a lot of sharing with him, and he and I were good friends. He's not yet a Christian, but he understands where I come from in terms of God. I said, 'Jim, all I'd have to do is poke my head up and a bullet would hit me right between the eyes.'"

Jim did not budge. He argued that during the Reagan and Bush years, because of their emphasis on keeping government out of private life, the NEA had been left to some loose cannons, whose stances even more typically liberal artists did not like. Now, Clinton was vowing to reexamine the role of the NEA. America's artists, Jim argued, needed a fellow artist in there who would defend funding beauty in the arts over exploitative political and social messages; someone who would be willing to take the heat.

Later, back in Texas, the subject came up in passing with Texas state senator Nancy MacDonald, a liberal whom Bill opposed politically, but with whom he shared a mutual love of art. In fact, she owned some of his paintings. To Bill's surprise, MacDonald said that Bill was the guy for the job and wrote a glowing letter of recommendation, urging Governor Ann Richards to nominate Bill. The senator said, in part, that Bill is a "thoughtful mature artistic talent" whose "fine talent blends with his innate and most unusual ability to discern and emphasize the relationship of today's important events with the roots of the human race."

Richards then highly recommended Bill to President Clinton. Other Texas congressmen jumped on board; liberals and conservatives alike all over the country started pushing for his nomination. In the process, Bill wrote a paper entitled "Change and the National Endowment for the Arts." In it, he stressed that the NEA existed to support national progress and scholarship in the arts. He said that support from the private sector was fundamental. He argued that certain paintings, exhibits, and productions funded in recent years by the NEA have been off base and poor art.

> While the NEA must not impose a single aesthetic standard or attempt to direct artistic content, it should not sacrifice the pursuit

of excellence for the sake of poorly executed diversity. Nothing drains vitality from the quest for artistic excellence more than the knowledge that superior works go unrewarded because inferior art, whose principal attribute is diversity, is receiving the taxpayer's funds. Emphasis must be placed on excellence and diversity, not one at the expense of the other.

Changes must be made by taking politics out of the NEA. We must return art to the task of serving art, rather than art becoming a platform for political agendas. ...

The NEA should not fund that which taxpayers consistently and persistently reject. The NEA is not a welfare agency for artists who decide to refuse to be accountable to the public interest. It must stand for excellence. ... How can Americans ever enthusiastically support the NEA if grants are given to artists who persistently and consistently defame ethnic or religious beliefs? There are existing institutions and foundations which can support such causes, but the NEA should not be one of them.

My objective is to fulfill the original interest of the NEA through three necessary changes:

1. NEA art will not be associated with any political agenda.
2. NEA funds will no longer "bless" what the public curses.
3. NEA activities will win unparalleled financial support from the American taxpayer.

Bill Herring, underground Christian, becomes Bill Herring—mountaintop prophet! Even Christian media watcher Donald Wildmon of the American Family Association, who has logged many an hour writing nasty letters to the NEA, could stand up and applaud. Ironically, Bill is not exactly a fan of Wildmon's or of any of the so-called religious right. Between Bill and Wildmon, whom do you think might have the most long-term positive effect on art and culture?

Bill says that too many Christians are cut away from the culture and cannot speak to it, or they just simply are too scared: "Someone has said that silence is golden; but more often than not, silence is yellow." In typical Texas fashion, Bill says it is time for believers to "walk into the night and start kicking cockroaches in the butt." The key is walking *into* the night, not standing on the perimeter.

"I believe that Christians need to go into the world and in order to do that in our society, they may have to put their wedding rings on the other hand, to run the risk of being rejected by Christians in order to relate to non-Christians. It is dangerous, but it is even more dangerous for the Christian not to. Have you ever looked at someone who is anemic? Have you looked at their skin color? Have you looked at their eyes? I see this too much. The last thing I want to do is face the consequences of seeing that in my mirror. This I know. I want to die well. And dying well means that I live with no regrets."

As God has brought Bill success and prestige, Bill continues to speak of and demonstrate his faith. Currently, he does a fair amount of travel, speaking out and conducting artists' workshops. In his publicity literature, he expressly states that he "works primarily with disenfranchised individuals, especially women, who seek the skills necessary for greatness on the American art scene." As a teacher, Bill has a passionate drive to give his talents and his successes back to his Creator—to reinvent them in others.

He has also accumulated his share of detractors. One person, obviously a Christian, angrily wrote three legal-sized pages— unsigned—after reading that he had been considered to run the NEA. (By the way, he was edged out by actress Jane Alexander, but is currently being considered for the National Council for the Arts.)

"It kind of made me bleed a little," Bill says of the harsh letter. "The person said, 'You've sold out. You've joined the other camp. You're playing with spiritual fire.' The person said, 'The name of Christ has been polluted because of what you've done. The NEA has so offended humanity and life itself that for someone of your stature, and what you say and believe, for you to be headed in that direction means that you've abandoned the very things you've always stood for.'"

Bill has come to terms with the fact that he will not always be understood, and that he will be criticized not only by non-Christians but also by believers. He sees the whole scenario like a game of marbles where a group of boys kneel at the taw line, shooting their mouths off about whose marbles are the best and who can shoot the best— i.e., what the right Christian thing to do is and what it is not. "The taw line is where you step out of the talk game and get into the walk game. You put your finger on that line and you either shoot or you don't. And when people shoot, only one comes out a winner. You can't really know the pain of rejection until you step up to the taw line. I realize that I'm going to have enemies, and I have enemies. I have significant enemies. I suspect that I'm going to have more."

Such is the risk one runs for standing up for age-old principles in a rough-and-tumble world. Bill derives peace from knowing that God loves him. "Because I have that, I have everything I need. So I don't look for love from other people. I'm able to live off his love."

Bill recently published a polished book of sketches accompanied by his thoughts on art, creativity, and life. It is full of quotes and guidance that he has accumulated from various thinkers and artists throughout his years of reading and painting. In it he talks about thinking for oneself, about daring to be different, about how to perform at peak, about dreaming big dreams, about feeding the artist's fire, about achieving greatness. He discusses life as one artist would with another artist.

Those who read the book are also subtly counseled to care for their families before feeding their careers: "Get your marriage squared away before you start gambling," he advises. They are told where true greatness comes from: "Nobody can compete with a genuine gift from God," he asserts. Toward the end of the book, is Bill's opinion on what life boils down to: There, beside a spectacularly somber sketch of timeless mother with child, Bill writes, "We will not meet the baby—but the King. Are you ready?"

One morning Bill walked out in his backyard. The sky above was pure blue, the color artists associate with expanding the mind. The grass beneath him was lush and green, the most soothing of colors. He plugged in the sound score from the movie *The Last of the Mohicans* and turned it up loud. Then he got out a group of tear sheets of beautiful American models and put them on the seat next to him. He drew in contemplation. When he finished that, he drew both of his dogs in the ridiculous positions they assumed as they basked in the sunshine. Next, he made coffee, the smell of which was magnificent, and simply enjoyed the great thrill of creating something beautiful out of nothing. "That's my job. I get up in the morning and my job is to take nothing and to make something of it."

In a sense, that is the call of every serious Christian. He notes, "The whole issue of the Christian life should go back to the fact that you live in such a way that men cannot hold themselves back from asking you what's going on. Not because you issue them protest letters or put signs over your door or the little fish symbol on your car windshield, but because they sense life there and it is attractive— like a fresh yellow blossom on a drab-green desert shrub when the light hits it just right."

Bill sounds like a pretty tough west Texas hombre, and he is, but I can also testify that he is a very loving, kind, and considerate friend. To get a letter from a friend is always a treat; to get a letter from Bill Herring is pure joy. Not only are his letters full of Scripture and wise counsel lovingly, almost shyly, given, they are gloriously amplified with compelling drawings and sketches that he has done just for you. Every letter is a thrill.

Johnny Hart

My correspondence is doubly blessed. Letters from Bill Herring with their artistic adornments are very special. I also get letters adorned with a strange caveman and a sly wizard. They are a delight and will always be treasured.

Johnny Hart is a visual artist whose medium for more than thirty-six years has been the comics. Daily he sits in his personal studio staring face-to-face with that caveman and that wizard. Ink pens clutter his table. Paper carpets his floor. Characters from his famous comic strips—*B.C.* and *The Wizard of Id*—can be seen throughout the room, alongside an array of awards and honors.

It is another workday for one of America's most revered cartoonists.

The gray, sixty-three-year-old gag man (his own description) gazes out a sun-soaked window at part of the one-hundred-and-fifty-acre spread that writing and drawing *B.C.* and the *Wizard* has allowed him to purchase. Shade trees gently sway in the breeze. Reflections of clouds dance across his thirty-acre lake, replete with a boathouse.

For years, Hart has been perched atop the cartooning world. He believes that the Lord put him there for a reason. And every prudent chance he gets, Hart intends to take advantage of it. One particular day the phone rang. The voice on the line was Mike Peters, a member of the loose fraternity of well-known cartoonists with whom Hart socializes. Peters draws the nationally famous strip, *Mother Goose & Grimm.*

"You know, Johnny," Peters, who is somewhat of a liberal, moaned, "I got up early this morning and sat there for three hours, and I couldn't think of a thing to draw."

Exasperation oozed through the receiver. Hart could feel it. He quickly thought, and then offered this analysis: "The devil is only playing games with you," he said.

What!? Would Johnny Hart dare to insert the realm of the spiritual into the big-money realm of syndicated newspapers, an arena long thought to be almost devoid of spiritual concern? Yes, he would—and he regularly and nonchalantly does.

"The devil is a very real entity, and that's the way he operates," Johnny continued to a listening Peters. "What you should do is a joke or gag against the devil in your strip."

Laughter suddenly filled the phone lines between rural Endicott, New York, and Sarasota, Florida.

"That's a great idea," *Mother Goose & Grimm*'s creator replied. "And you know, when I'm up there for the B.C. Golf Open (a yearly PGA event at which Johnny entertains some of America's top cartoonists), I want to talk to you about these things."

"Okay," said Hart. "I look forward to it."

"These things," as Peters put it, are what drives Hart the most nowadays. Ever since 1987 when he and his wife Bobby made a conscious decision to walk with Christ, Hart's life and cartooning have been guided by his relationship with the Lord.

Perhaps Peters thought Johnny was joking when he suggested doing a *gag* (Hart's term for a great comic strip) on the devil; but it is likely that he knows Hart well enough to realize that *B.C.*'s creator meant exactly what he said. "I find myself trying to put the Gospel into practically every strip I create without being obvious about it," Johnny says without apology.

Johnny will tell you that that is what good cartooning is all about—getting a message through to people via a subtle twist. When the reader sees it, it causes a *spasm* (Johnny's term for catching a reader with a fresh look at an old truth). That sounds much like what any good preacher would hope for—shedding fresh light on old truth, not to mention causing a holy spasm in the listener.

Johnny is a master of the art. More than that, he is a study of a Christian artist committed to excellence. Do not take my word for it. Just look at what his secular colleagues have said about him:

- Best Humor Strip in America (six-times), The National Cartoonist Society
- The Reuben (Cartoonist of the Year), The National Cartoonist Society
- The Yellow Kid Award (for Best Cartoonist), The International Congress of Comics
- The Sam Adamson Award (twice), Sweden's international award for graphic artists
- The Elsie Segar Award, King Features Syndicate

Recently, Johnny was going back through some old strips, looking for an original to give to a charity auction. "Much to my surprise, every other one had some kind of a statement—either a conservative political message or touching some aspect of religious life."

When Hart first began consciously inserting such messages in his strips, he started getting letters. Many of them were from stunned Christians. "People would say, 'Wow, how did you dare do that?' like I had committed some kind of sin or crime. Others would say, 'How did you get away with that? Boy, you must be brave.'" Hart calls this kind of attitude "pathetic."

"I formed a symbolic image of today's Christians in their little homes, the old 1950s-style home, peaking out from behind the doors on the edge of a large window." They were timid, worried, little people, as Hart recalls them.

But the way in which Hart reads the Scriptures, Christians are to go into all of the world with the Gospel message. "Some people try to make me into a hero for speaking through a newspaper syndicate, but I don't see it that way. Too many Christians have bought into the lie that we shouldn't mention our beliefs."

And in some cases, the way Hart witnesses does not fit some Christians' image of a Christian witness. One case in point harkens back to Christmas of 1990. As is Hart's tradition, on the special Christian days of the calendar he tries to put an extra emphasis on Christ into his strips. This particular year he thought he had found a gag with a twist that should really make non-Christians think about Christ and the Gospel. Here's the strip:

By permission of Johnny Hart and Creators Syndicate, Inc.

Granted, the twist at the end uses strong language, but the message delivered to anyone who paused long enough was clear: The Good News of Jesus Christ has the effect of driving the hell and sin out of the life of believers.

Unfortunately, one group of activist Christian leaders never paused to consider the dynamic message Johnny had delivered to his audience, most of whom are unbelievers and would surely be appropriately stunned to think of hell in its real sense, as opposed to their normal, vulgar sense. Donald Wildmon of the American Family Association mailed the strip out to three thousand evangelical pastors with a red-flag warning that Hart was blaspheming God.

Suddenly, Hart started getting letters en masse. They were all terribly similar, using the same buzzwords and phrases. He finally learned that Wildmon was behind this all-out assault on his work.

What a sad picture. But all too often it is a very real one. There are two camps among evangelicals in America today. One camp is so ready to criticize and bash the message and the messengers of the mainstream media that they cannot pause, even for a moment, to recognize the Gospel's being delivered creatively, rolled up on their front doorsteps. These guys seldom get it. The money, effort, and goodwill that they waste is enormous.

They make it hard for people like Hart who realize that fulfilling Christ's call to take the Gospel into all the world, including media and the arts, means a mandate to be fresh and creative. Hart's type recognizes that the Gospel does beat the hell out of people, and that it is no crime for an artist to use words or images to ingeniously get this point over to people who would not crack the door of a church to hear the Gospel presented in a traditional way from the pulpit. This is called being salt—being a lamb among wolves.

Who needs enemies when you have friends, right?

Well, in Johnny's case, as usual, he was most gracious about the criticism he received from fellow brothers and sisters about trying to share Christ with the world. "I personally wrote every person back who had written me," Johnny recalls. And this is what he said:

> In a world influenced by principalities, powers, rulers of the darkness of this world and wicked spirits in heavenly places, one does not win popularity contests witnessing to the Gospel. Regular readers of my two comic strips, however, will tell you that as often as possible, I try to do just that. Sometimes it is achieved with great subtlety, and sometimes when the message seems important enough, I may resort to cheap gimmickry to draw attention to it. In the *B.C.* Christmas strip of 1990, I tried to draw attention to the oft overlooked fact that Jesus came into the earth to destroy the works of the devil (1 John 3:8). That sweet little baby lying in an animal feeding trough in a stable in Bethlehem would one day emerge glorified out of the pit of hell with the keys to the gates in his hand. The Bible says he made an open show of his victory over Satan (Col. 2:15). This triumph over evil and death is the legacy of all Christians. It was the message implied in the *B.C.* Christmas strip, a message not just of hope, but of victory. The use of the crude figure of speech, *Beats the hell out of me,* was the gimmick employed as the attention grabber. Unfortunately, a few readers, one even a member of the clergy, never got past the figure of speech and berated me for blaspheming my Lord. To those who were offended, I apologize for initiating the misunderstanding that caused you to be offended. In hindsight, I suppose I should have used, "It beats the devil out of me!" But then it would have just made sense.
>
> With love,
> Johnny Hart

Wow! Now there is the Gospel in word and deed.

Numerous Christians rewrote Johnny, apologizing and saying that they would watch for *B.C.* in the future. To his credit, Donald Wildmon himself wrote back to say in part: "My opponents always accuse me of being wrong. This time they are right."

Johnny Hart knows what being a Christian in the media means. It means having to be the best you can possibly be, since you are often scrutinized the most. And it means not only seeking to creatively share your faith with unbelievers but also seeking to kindly and patiently increase the awareness of believers that the media and art are not off-limits, and that Christians can and must speak through them.

Johnny Hart believes that the Lord placed him atop the cartooning world for a reason. Knowing that makes it easier to take the barbs—Christian and non-Christian—like when the *Los Angeles Times* repeatedly pulls one of his strips because it contains a message of morality. Once, Hart recalls, "I told Rick Newcombe, president of my syndicate, Creator's Syndicate, to just take my strip out of the *L.A. Times* because I didn't need them."

Newcombe convinced Hart to wait awhile longer, that a new editor was taking over the *Times'* comics department, one who might be more friendly to Hart's message. Hart agreed.

Such are the tensions that routinely confront Hart. But there are the more personal challenges too—for instance, Rick Newcombe himself. Rick and Johnny go back to when Rick helped run the syndicate that Johnny had his two strips with for years previously. When that syndicate was bought out, Rick was about to be shifted to a do-nothing job.

Instead, Rick decided to launch his own syndicate, a lifelong dream. Johnny, who owns his strips, was right there to support him. He decided to move *B.C.* to Rick's new Creator's Syndicate; he left *The Wizard of Id* with the old syndicate for five years as a good-faith gesture to the new management, who came to respect Johnny for his upright business dealings.

Nowadays, both strips are with Rick's syndicate. And it is not uncommon for the two men—the Christian and the former believer—to have long talks. Not long ago, during one of their talks, Rick told Johnny, "I'm not a doubter anymore, thanks to my mother, my two brothers, and *even you.*"

And you can be sure of one thing: *B.C.* and *The Wizard of Id* will be right there waiting for Rick if and when he crosses over into newness of life.

Can Christ use artists in the secular world? The answer screams out at us when we look at Johnny Hart's life. *B.C.'s* and the *Wizard's* creator speaks to millions daily through his comics. (One woman wrote to say that the message in one *Wizard* strip prevented her from committing suicide that day.) Hart brings light into the often dark Sunday news. People who do not go to church on Sunday do go to the comic pages.

Beyond that, the mere fact that Johnny has achieved such status among his peers gives him a platform to share the Good News with them. "It isn't always easy," he says. Still, he has a dream: "Ultimately, one day every gag in the comics will be a Christian gag."

Until then, Johnny Hart will remain one of God's choicest lambs, roaring loudly across miles and miles of newsprint.

✳

Does the story of Bill Bippus inspire you? We must continue to strive, at the college level, to cultivate people who have the talent to make the visual arts their ministry. Only then will it be possible for more Christians to make a difference in this vital area, just as Bill Herring and Johnny Hart have already done. Charge on, lambs!

2

Lambs and the Theater: Dramatic Boards

When I wrote *Roaring Lambs,* I knew so little about Christians in the theater that I neglected the entire area. As a fan of Broadway, the London stage, and quality regional theater, I was certainly aware of the power and the possibility of theater. I was simply ignorant of what God's people were doing in this important culture-shaping medium. I did not know there were lambs among the wolves of greasepaint and stage lights. Thankfully, I now know a little more, enough at least to introduce you to some of the very talented, very committed Christians who are seeking to be salt and light as actors, writers, and producers of theatrical productions that point people to the Savior and glorify him. They inspire me. I hope they will you as well.

Steve Rue

Steve Rue is a hero. He is a young man who lives on the plains of Kansas far from any of the country's showbiz centers. He has no organization, no outside backing, and no significant personal wealth. What he does have is talent, a desire—make that a *need*—to serve, and a great deal of faith. The sum of what he has adds up to a great deal. He does not pay very much attention to what he does not have.

What Steve Rue has done is to write a God-honoring musical play, *The Ram in the Thicket.* Writing an original full-length musical drama is, in and of itself, a significant and praiseworthy feat, but it was not enough for Steve. He wanted people to see, hear, and be

impacted by his play. So, undeterred by what he did not have, and
calling on the resources he did have, mainly his abundant faith, he
set about to stage and produce the show for audiences in and around
Kansas. People came. People applauded. People were moved. Steve
was still not satisfied—his work needed to be seen by a broader
audience. So, he did what any red-blooded American Christian
would do. He took his show to New York—and not only to New
York, but to a recognized off-Broadway theater.

I wish that I was a talented enough writer to get across to you
the enormity of Steve Rue's accomplishment. Many, many more-
experienced writers and producers with significant monetary backing try for years to have their work produced off-Broadway and do
not succeed. What Steve accomplished is truly the stuff of show business legend and lore. For a first-time writer to take his work and open
it in an off-Broadway theater without a star-power cast or a promotional or advertising budget and to complete a successful run is, to use
show business jargon, stupendous, colossal, and mind-boggling.

How did he do it? God honored his faith and his effort. Steve is
now back in Kansas working on his next production. I can hardly
wait to see what he and the Lord will do next.

The Steve Rue story has many lessons for all of us. First, we need to
recognize that the theater is one of those important cultural-shaping
areas in which Christians need to be deeply and productively involved
at all levels. There is absolutely no reason why Steve or other Christians
should not be showcased in the largest, most prestigious theaters *on*
Broadway, and off Broadway and in regional theaters.

As always, parents, churches, and our Christian colleges have
vital roles to play. We need to show our young people in very deliberate, ongoing, organized ways how they can serve the Lord in the
area of theater if that is the direction in which their calling and talents lead. We need to ready a steady supply of lambs to begin serving among the wolves of this important area of our culture.

Every church should have someone in charge of the body's efforts in this area. This person and his or her committee should, as a minimum, be engaged in

1. making sure the "Steve Rues" are supported;
2. organizing church excursions to see worthwhile productions;
3. bringing professional Christian actors and other theater-related professionals to speak and hold seminars at the church;
4. bringing Christian production companies and/or one person shows to perform, depending on the size of the church;
5. staging at least one in-church dramatic production a year;
6. building a church scholarship fund to help support the education of church young people who are called to serve the Lord through the theater;
7. having a theatrical outreach to schools, hospitals, retirement homes, and so forth.

Thankfully, at least some of our Christian colleges already have high-quality drama programs. Seattle Pacific University is showcased later in this chapter. I am proud to say that my own alma mater, Greenville College, has an excellent drama department, which stages several high-quality productions each year. As good as these programs are, though, their sights need to be raised. They should have as one of their announced goals the preparation of professionals of the top rank who are committed to a life of ministry through the theater and to the people of the theater.

As in all areas of Christian involvement with the arts, we need trained, high-quality Christian support staff for those who actually do the performing. One of the most important lessons I have learned since *Roaring Lambs* is how badly God's creative people need the help of Christians who have business and financial acumen. As it is, far too many of the church's best creative talents spend far too much of their time and energy on logistical business and financial concerns. We need to support the Steve Rues a great deal better in this regard. Our Christian colleges should develop curricula to meet this need.

Dennis Babcock

With thanksgiving we can say that there are many other heroic lambs, besides hero Steve Rue, in the theatrical world among the wolves. There certainly are not enough, but we can be grateful for ones like Dennis Babcock, a nationally recognized theatrical producer. During his career, Dennis has produced shows featuring Princess Grace, Henry Fonda, James Whitmore, Joel Grey, Julie Harris, Hume Cronyn, and Jessica Tandy. Musicians he has produced include Neil Sedaka, Melissa Manchester, the Talking Heads, and Devo. With producer/actor/writer Leonard Nimoy, Babcock created and produced an internationally acclaimed production of the life of Vincent Van Gogh, *Vincent*. In 1981, he was the executive producer of the ABC Television Arts and Entertainment filming of the same show, which still runs on cable TV and is available on Paramount Home Video.

While Steve Rue is, perhaps, the ultimate theatrical beginner, Dennis Babcock is, perhaps, the ultimate professional theatrical veteran. We can be deeply thankful for both. Their goals are the same—to serve the Lord Jesus. There is a significant scene at the end of the first act of Dennis Babcock's well-known production of *A Christmas Carol*, Charles Dickens' story that has long been in the public domain and revised by scores of writers and producers. In Babcock's version, very true to the book's original 1843 form, Scrooge has just been confronted by the Ghost of Christmas Past. He is pondering a life full of horrible, selfish decisions. One by one, characters stroll past a semidelirious Scrooge, who is sitting on the stage's lonely dark edge. As they pass, each character throws out one cutting comment after another—all aspersions that the money monger had cast their way. Draped in darkness and hazy fog, a tormented, terrified Scrooge bemoans his bad life—not a whole lot different from the inner life of many a theater actor.

But there is more going on in this scene, at least the way that Babcock plays it. The characters form a semicircle chorus around the pitiful miser. As he begins to scream out, "Why?! Why?!" the growing chorus around him, their words thinly and hauntingly perceptible, sing lines from an old English hymn, "Christmas Bells: Tell all the world, Jesus is King! Tell all the world, Jesus is King!"

It is exceptional theater—the message suggested, not hammered. Nonetheless, thousands of theatergoers who have seen Babcock's much-heralded version of *A Christmas Carol* are appropriately confronted at Christmas with a universal question: "Why?!" The answer to this and all human questions: "Jesus is King!"

Dennis Babcock, who is forty-six, knows what he is talking about. Dennis had professional respect, and he had money. Yet he once was suffocated by his own taunting *Why?* chorus, tangled as he was in the middle of what he calls "the crazy entertainment industry." "That is exactly what I asked the Lord when I was lying in the hospital after years of cocaine and worldly living. I asked, 'Why am I here? Why can't I kick this?' It's just nuts," says Babcock, who for several years managed one of the nation's premier regional theaters, the Guthrie Theater in Minneapolis. Babcock found the answer, but he has never forgotten the question, one he knows constantly torments most actors, producers, and stagehands.

Now Dennis wants to be a facilitator for truth. He wants to help others answer the *Why?* question. In 1986, he left the Guthrie and launched his own production company, Palm Tree Productions. Then, in 1993, he fulfilled a dream by creating another company, Christmas Carol, Inc. During his years at the Guthrie, Dennis had supervised the production of one of the most-copied versions ever of Dickens' Christmas classic. Thousands of Minneapolis and St. Paul residents have considered it a staple part of their Christmas observance for years. To his surprise, Dennis discovered that only a handful of other cities had their own yearly production of *A Christmas Carol*. Furthermore, in reading Dickens' original version, Dennis was struck by the author's clear metaphorical portrayal of a man undergoing a conversion experience. Dickens went so far as to intimate that Christ is the ultimate answer as seen in his references to the North Star and "that holy (Christmas) night."

Suddenly, a lightbulb went off. Dennis thought: *Wouldn't it be wonderful to take this story—with its real intent—to cities around the nation at the quality level of the famous Guthrie?* So, this past Christmas of 1994, the second year that Christmas Carol, Inc., has been in operation, Babcock's version of the classic story was staged in Albany, New York, and Philadelphia, Pennsylvania. Each year the company will add another city to its tour.

The first day of production in Albany, 1993, Dennis was in a stew. For days, he had felt that somehow, gently and respectfully (two key words for Dennis), he should relate to his cast and crew of one hundred (including Wilford Brimley of Quaker Oats commercial fame), what Christ meant to him. He was nervous. He had even had trouble sleeping. His wife, well-known Minneapolis-St. Paul TV anchor, Diana Pierce, encouraged him to relax and trust the Lord.

There had been a flurry of activity around him when he arrived at the theater. A buzz was in the air. The set designer, who had staged for Sir Lawrence Olivier's *Hamlet* and had won awards for *Rosencrantz and Guildenstern are Dead*, was present. Dennis's well-known London director was peering his way. Carpenters, lighting technicians, actors—everyone gathered in the rehearsal hall awaiting a tone-setting word from their producer. Dennis was brief. He welcomed everyone; said how exciting it was to actually begin rehearsals after four, long tough years of seeking the show's financing and encouraged everyone to do their best. Then, in closing, Dennis said to the mixed cast of believers and nonbelievers: "If you would allow me please. I don't mean to proselytize here or to offend anyone. But it's important to me to share with you who my boss is. So I'd like to pray and ask him to start us off." He ended his prayer in Jesus' name, and off they went.

Later, during the production's run, one actor approached Dennis: "You know, I really appreciate the fact that you started this thing off with prayer." Another woman rededicated her life to Christ while the production was running, after attending a local gathering of Media Fellowship International that Dennis helps lead.

Dennis is not out there yelling in people's ears with a director's megaphone or spotlighting them with a stage light and then shooting Jesus at them while they are blinded. He is being real and doing excellent work. In Dennis's case, his battle cry is: gently and respectfully. "I keep coming back to those two words," he says. Dennis recalls how uncomfortable he always was in the theater when people would cold witness to him. Furthermore, he reads in 1 Peter 3:15 that Christians should "always be ready to give an answer to everyone who asks you, to give the reason for the hope that you have. But do this with gentleness and respect." Dennis wants to live his life in the secular theater in such a way that people are dying to ask him, "Hey, what is it with you?"

In 1987, when Dennis left the Guthrie Theater and formed Palm Tree Productions, he wanted "to produce and promote various theater, film, television, and entertainment" that met one or more of the following criteria. The shows should "enrich life, furnish a pattern for imitation, summon others to their tasks, show the reality and results of faith, and honor and respect God." *A Christmas Carol*, although created and produced by Dennis's second company, fits that goal.

Dennis carries a business card in his pocket. On it is the corporate name—Palm Tree Productions, Inc.—followed by his own name. "Sooner or later," he says, "someone asks me why I named the company Palm Tree." That is a logical question since Dennis lives in Minnesota. And that is when this highly regarded theatrical producer asks them, gently and respectfully: "Do you *really* want to know?" If they say yes, then Dennis hands them a second business card. It reads:

Since you asked—The palm is a symbol of victory and triumph.

Psalm 92:12, 14–15: "The righteous shall flourish like the palm tree. . . . They shall bring forth fruit in old age; they shall be fat and flourishing . . . to show that the Lord is upright. He is our rock, and there is no unrighteousness in him (KJV)."

This company is founded on the above principles.

Thanks for asking.

That is Dennis Babcock, a roaring lamb.

Scott Nolte

"It would be strange if the outstanding theater event in Seattle's summer of '92 was a little musical staged in the basement of a North End church. But *Smoke on the Mountain*, a Taproot Theatre production at the Fairview Church, will be hard to beat. It's touching. It has catchy, accessible music. It is warm and hopeful. It has interesting characters. It has a simple, engaging plot. The actors, singers, and musicians act, sing, and play well." So begins a rave review by the theater critic of the *Seattle Post-Intelligencer*. Would you go to see a show with a review like that? I would. Meet some more heroic roaring lambs of the theater.

Taproot is the culmination of a vision held by a group of theater majors from a Christian university, Seattle Pacific. For more than eighteen years, under the leadership of Scott Nolte, they have been staging productions in and around Seattle that speak of high ideals, and they do it with such excellence that the whole city has taken notice.

"The modern theater has been very good at trying to expose humanities' shortcomings and our pain by the flaws in our society," says Taproot founder Scott Nolte in a 1994 *Seattle Post-Intelligencer* article. He adds: "But we [in the theater] haven't really been good at saying what the solutions are. That's what we are trying to do. We sometimes describe ourselves as a theater of hope. We want to show the consequences of what happens when you do have hope."

The thirty-nine-year-old Nolte, a 1976 graduate of Seattle Pacific, is articulate. He is also persistent. Building a theater company from scratch, straight out of a Christian school, is not the easiest thing in the world. After years of producing plays and musicals in a church auditorium (a former high school auditorium), Taproot is on the verge of settling in a permanent location. After years of fund-raising ($770,000 is the total goal) and the support of a large number of patrons, Nolte now sits in his makeshift office, which once served as the women's rest room for an X-rated Seattle movie house. The pounding and growl of heavy machinery can be heard through his door where workers are gutting and renovating the old theater so it can be a permanent residence for Taproot. Work should be finished in 1995. The building sits smack in a neighborhood on the brink of decline. By design, Taproot hopes that their presence will stimulate the economy and infuse spiritual life into the tired area. Talk about being redemptive. Talk about being lambs among wolves.

From his office, Scott recalls how, in 1982, after several successful early years, the local and national economy shifted. His staff was reduced from eight to three in no time, and Nolte and his actress wife Pam were ready to "throw in the towel, sell our home, and start a bed-and-breakfast somewhere." But something would not release them from their vision of a positive value-laden theater in Seattle, Washington, a city in a state neither of which are known for being highly churched. The Noltes stuck with their vision, and in just months Taproot was back on its feet with a larger staff than before.

That same year, Scott was looking for an older actor to fill a leading role in *You Can't Take It with You*. His usual Christian connections came up dry. Then he met Renn, a former Hollywood actor and producer with immense talent that was balanced by a wonderful gentleness. There was a slight problem though. Renn practiced a mix of Baha'i, Transcendental Meditation, and Religious

Science. In other words, a not too untypical example of what you might find in Seattle's artistic community. Although Scott basically resisted casting non-Christians, he felt peace in casting Renn.

In the ensuing two years, Scott cast Renn three more times. One evening, Renn called Scott and Pam at home. "Can I come by? I'd like to talk to you about accepting Jesus Christ as my Savior." That night, on a softly lit back porch, Renn found his true spiritual home.

Years later, Renn came back to work for Taproot in *Both Your Houses*. As Scott was about to start rehearsals one night, Renn came over and told him that his doctor had scheduled a series of tests to track some potentially serious symptoms that he was having. Scott could sense Renn's fear and knew what needed to be done. He opened rehearsal that night with this: "You all have different points of reference on Taproot's work—but one thing we do is care about one another." He told everyone—a mix of Christian and non-Christian actors, stage carpenters, and technicians—about Renn's health situation. Then they all circled Renn and prayed.

What a difference that night made. Not only was Renn moved and strengthened, but others were captivated by the experience as well. A guest lighting director who had worked at two hundred theaters in the U.S. and Canada told Scott, "Your company is the only one that doesn't stress me out and ruin my life." At one point, that man's wife asked the question every Christian from Dennis Babcock to Michael W. Smith prays to hear: "What's different about you guys?" And another actor recommitted his life to Christ the very night that they prayed with Renn. Still another nonbelieving member of the company filed the experience with Renn away in his head. Later, he called Scott after seeing the Taproot production of *Godspell*. He said that he had been reading his Bible and asked Scott some deep questions about God and life.

Renn died in October 1992 of cancer. But his testimony of need and faith helped bring others closer to God. As Scott notes, this is a facet of Taproot that is personal, casual, and spontaneous; it cannot be measured or quantified.

Much more is occurring in the broader community due to the company's faithfulness to excellence in theater. Besides doing inspirational theater in local churches, Taproot members have produced hundreds of original plays for more than five hundred thousand school children. The dramas deal with chemical abuse and recovery as well as adolescent sexuality and abstinence. Anyone who knows Seattle at all, knows that it is the center of the grunge counterculture, made up of thousands of homeless, dropout teens who are devoted to hard-driving, alternative rock music and drugs. Kurt Cobain of Seattle-based Nirvana, who committed suicide in 1994, represents this sad, needy bunch of kids. Through their appearances at local schools, Taproot's creative staff of musicians and actors have been able to encourage many children to steer clear of this promiscuous drug scene.

But the company's effect on the local culture has not stopped there. In 1994, Taproot staged *The Cottonpatch Gospel*. It consists of just four supporting actors and Scott, who plays a Southern countrified version of Jesus. At one point, Scott's Jesus character says, "Come unto me, all of you who have had a bellyful of emptiness. Get in the harness with me." What a powerful message for the lost and lonely children strewn through Seattle's streets. One night at the end of the show, a woman approached Scott. She took his face in her hands and kissed him on the cheek. Scott could see her hurting heart. "Do you know what you have here?" she asked. Her son was dying of AIDS. She wanted to go and tell him and all his friends to come see the play and experience Jesus in all his humanity and compassion.

Nolte and his staff believe that good theater can pierce hard hearts and help mend broken areas. They believe in excellence. They do not compromise on quality. Still there have been times when representing a company that strives to thoroughly reflect Christ has been hard. For instance, Taproot once staged a production of *The Nerd*, a story of friendship and individuality in the life of a geeky, bumbling guy. For Taproot's version, Scott cut sixty-one curse words and off-color jokes. He kept the bad characters bad and allowed some of their language and habits to reflect that, which, after all, is life, and theater portrays life. Scott was comfortable with the final product. Many loved the production. One person said, "Thanks for the excellent cutting of the nerd's cursings." But others were angry. One complained, "How dare you! Who gave you the right to cut the swearing out of *The Nerd*?" Such is the tension Scott and his friends feel as Christians performing in a secular culture. It is always so when lambs are among the wolves.

❋

Steve Rue, Dennis Babcock, and Scott Nolte are certainly not all of God's people who work for him and represent him in theatrical pursuits—not by a long shot. We have in no way tried to be inclusive, only representative. My ignorance remains vast about the theater generally and about all that God is doing in and through it. I hope that these people have whet your appetite for Christian theater.

3

Lambs and Journalism: Front-Page News

The lamb currently roaring the loudest in journalism is not even a member of that profession. He does not live in any of the glamorous media centers—not in New York, Washington, D.C., or Los Angeles. He runs a small business and lives in the rather prosaic midwestern city of Lansing, Michigan. He has not had any specialized training or education and has no extraordinary talents or skills. His story should be a blessing, an encouragement, and a challenge to all of us who seek to make a difference for God and his kingdom. It certainly should make those of us who think we have excuses for not serving very uncomfortable.

Jim Russell

While Jim Russell may have no specialized training or education and no extraordinary talents or skills, he is not an ordinary person—not by any standard of measurement. What sets him apart and puts him in such a specialized, even rarefied, category, is his amazing love for Jesus and his passion to do the Master's will. I have been around the block a few times and only rarely have I known anyone who takes his commitment to serve more seriously. When Jesus admonished us to be salt, for Jim it was not an option to be considered but an order to be obeyed. He takes the Great Commission personally. He has no choice but to be about making disciples.

Before you conjure up a picture of Jim Russell as some sober, somber, otherworldly, saintlike character, be sure that you get a true glimpse of the man. He is a guy who is great fun to be with. He loves good jokes and is not above teasing me in almost every communication we have. He and his wife Phyllis are delightful dinner companions who know much about good food. Jim served two tours of duty in the Marine Corps. He flies his own plane and has been successful in the rough-and-tumble world of personally owned business. He takes service to the Lord very seriously, but he performs it with joy. This is not a contradiction in terms.

Now, how can I say that a sixty-nine-year-old small-business owner living in Lansing, Michigan, roars so loudly in the field of journalism? The question is even more appropriate when you consider the other lambs we know who are prominent in journalism—Peggy Wehmeyer of ABC; Frank Deford, often called the nation's best sportswriter; Cal Thomas, the hard-hitting, Scripture-quoting syndicated columnist and talk-show host; Edwin Pope, the Hall-of-Fame sports editor of the *Miami Herald*; Terry Mattingly, nationally syndicated Scripps-Howard religion columnist; Bill Murchison of Creator's Syndicate, who continually calls the nation back to righteousness in his column and now in his book, *Reclaiming Morality in America*; and Fred Barnes, the star of so many of the televised political panel shows. These are truly lambs among wolves. Jim Russell stands out even in this company because he has found a way to greatly magnify his voice, his roar. Because he has been obedient and faithful in following the leading of the Holy Spirit, he has a real direct hand in discipling the whole nation. And he is doing it through the so-called secular press. He is a journalist extraordinaire.

More than ten years ago, God gave Jim the vision to sponsor a journalism contest. This was to be a very special kind of journalism contest that would offer substantial cash prizes. To qualify, an article or feature had to first contain Scripture that was not tacked onto but fully integrated into the body of the piece. Second, but of equal importance, the piece must have run in a nonreligious, secular publication. In ten years, the contest, run by the Russells through their personal Amy Foundation, has become the most popular journalism contest in America. Every year, it receives thousands of entries, and the Amy Awards have recognized articles containing Scripture from publications as large as the *Wall Street Journal* to small town papers of very limited circulation. Winning entries have been written by famous writers with well-known bylines and by amateur writers who have been writing articles based in Scripture as a way to become roaring lambs themselves. The bottom line is that because of Jim's vision and obedience, millions more are impacted by God's Word than would otherwise be. And they often get it where they least expect it—from their daily paper.

The Amy Awards and all they accomplish for God's kingdom would by themselves qualify Jim Russell for a place in the Roaring Lambs Hall of Fame. But the Amy Awards may not be even the most significant and far-reaching of Jim's journalistic efforts. Inspired by the success of the Amy Awards and always sensitive to God's leading, in 1992, Jim began the Church Writing Group Movement. This wonderful effort seeks to tap the latent writing potential in America's 350,000 churches. It is based on the premise that almost anyone can write a letter to the editor of his local paper and, with the help and encouragement of a local group and the guidance of a national organization, many can write op-ed pieces, guest editorials, and features for a wide variety of publications.

The purpose of the Church Writing Group Movement is discipleship, not debate or polemics. It is about winning the hearts and minds of readers to the precepts of Jesus. To conform to Church Writing Group guidelines, an article must present Scripture in a loving, helpful way. As with the Amy Awards, a very important collateral benefit is that it gives church members an active, positive way to be engaged in being salt and light. Members who, for the most part, have been spectator Christians now feel that they have an active, ongoing ministry through their Church Writing Group activities.

The Church Writing Group Movement publishes a helpful newsletter, which is currently being sent free of charge to a mailing list of four thousand. There is also a videocassette available to anyone interested in forming other Church Writing Groups. In addition, detailed lesson plans enable local groups to be even more effective in discipling through journalism. Jim was kind enough to invite me to the first Church Writing Group conference and it was an exciting time. Writing Group members packed a large room at Michigan State University for a day of learning, inspiration, and lively interchange with professional journalists. More conferences are planned.

If you want more information about the Amy Writing Awards or the Church Writing Group Movement, write to: The Amy Foundation, P. O. Box 16091, Lansing, Michigan 48091. I hope you will agree that Jim Russell is a nonjournalist whose roar produces one of the sweetest possible sounds in that field.

Cal Thomas

It will not surprise you to know that Jim Russell is a friend and big fan of Cal Thomas. I am also very pleased to say that Cal is also a personal friend of mine. It was a great pleasure to formally induct him into the Roaring Lambs Hall of Fame in conjunction with the publication of his book, *The Things That Matter Most*. It is a great comfort to know that Cal is out there speaking and writing for many of us as he seeks to be the best servant of the Lord he can possibly be. His story is a thrilling one.

Cal Thomas had a day job with a well-known national Christian organization as their director of communications. But his heart and head said that God wanted him back in the thick of things in mainstream media, and by following that leading he has become one of the most prominent lambs among the wolves of journalism. Years ago, Thomas had been a rising star as a general assignment reporter for NBC News, working out of the company's Washington, D.C., office. Ever since his days as a teenage radio disc jockey doing "rip-and-read" news fresh off the wire, Thomas had known his calling was to be a journalist. He joined NBC's Washington staff at age eighteen, and his career took off. By his late twenties, he was doing up to ten stories a week for NBC, some locally and some nationally. His dream was to work in the highest echelons of American media.

In 1973 he lost his NBC job. But about the same time that his highest dream seemed to be crashing around him, the rest of Thomas's life was gaining a fresh new momentum. While still working with NBC, he and his wife began to feel their lives ring hollow. They began a search for what they call "significance and meaning." Cal was invited to a federal judge's prayer breakfast and heard someone speak about having a "personal faith in Jesus Christ." He was intrigued. Later he attended a Bible study led by Richard Halverson, then pastor of Fourth Presbyterian Church in suburban Washington and recently retired chaplain of the United States Senate. Halverson was reading from the *Living Bible*. Cal went out and bought one for himself. "I began to devour it," he says.

That night, he drove to his suburban Washington home, where a Bible study was in progress. Then and there, Cal made a turn from "making a god of my career to serving the true God."

Over the next few years, Cal was tutored by several Bible scholars and theologians, among them the respected Presbyterian scholar and advocate for Christians in culture, Dr. Francis Schaeffer. Cal spent time at Schaeffer's study center in L'Abri, Switzerland.

Then, after his stint with NBC and years of personal growth in faith, he was back in America working in communications for a Christian political activist organization. But what he had learned from Schaeffer about the importance of being in the culture and not removed from it kept tugging at him. He felt a strong urge to be where his voice would have a broader impact.

So what did Cal do? Sulk? Complain? No. He set about being salt and light right where he was. He set out to put his considerable communications talents and gifts into motion for God's kingdom. This is an important lesson for all of us to learn. The time to begin being obedient is now. The place to begin is wherever we find ourselves today. So many waste so much time and squander so many opportunities waiting until everything is just right. Cal began writing single-shot guest columns. On what some would call a whim, and others would call the Spirit's leading, he wrote a column and sent it off to what he regarded as the least likely paper to ever print it—the *New York Times*. "And in a burst of tolerance," cracks Cal, "they printed it." Often we have not because we ask not. Many Christians just cannot conceive of breaking into the *New York Times*. So our best articles go to *Christianity Today* or some other Christian publication. Lambs do not roar there.

A few months later, Cal wrote another column. This time he sent it to the *Washington Post*. They, too, printed his message. Then there was *USA Today*, and the *Washington Times*. Cal soon had nine or so finely tuned columns on political and social commentary that had appeared in some of America's finest papers. "I thought, *What's going on here? This is ruining my thinking about bias in the press.*"

Cal got an idea. He began packaging his columns and sending them out to various syndicates. Were they interested in a new columnist? he asked. Time and again Cal heard the same word—No. Running out of leads, Cal remembered an old friend who worked at the *Los Angeles Times* syndicate as vice president and chief copy editor.

Cal, known for being one cool cucumber, was a bit nervous that morning before his meeting with the *Los Angeles Times*. All his new hopes and dreams were riding on this. He prayed. During his prayer time, Cal knew that he had placed things in God's hands, something the old Cal Thomas of NBC days would never have done when it came to pushing for a career opportunity.

So there he was, in a restaurant, making small talk with two *Times* big hitters about life and leisure and, of course, journalism. After about an hour of conversation in which the two had clearly let Cal know that they had no more room in their syndicate's stable, the syndicate's vice president abruptly turned the conversation: "By the way," he said to Cal, "let's change the subject for a minute. You're a Christian, is that right?" Boom! There is that million dollar question again, the one that all the lambs among wolves find themselves fielding. The one we all ought to be prompting, and surely would be if only we were out there where the questioners are.

To be honest, the first thing Cal did upon hearing the question was to panic. After all, this looked like his last, best chance to get back into big-time mainstream media. Granted, it looked like the meeting was headed nowhere; but still he was not sure how direct he should be with his answer.

What do I do now? he moaned to himself. *If I am too forthcoming, it could kill any hope of success here.* Then and there, however, sitting in a restaurant with those media elite, his career seemingly dangling by a single strand of spaghetti, "A miraculous peace came over me," Cal recalls. "I told them all about my relationship with Jesus Christ and the difference it made in my life."

When he finished, his two attentive lunch mates glanced at each other.

"Isn't so-and-so leaving our syndication soon?" The copy editor asked her vice president.

"Yeah, he sure is," he replied. Then he turned to Cal: "Could you do two columns a week starting April 17?"

Just like that. Cal was back.

Cal is just as sure as he can be that God turned the hearts of those two for one main reason: Cal was not ashamed of the Gospel of Jesus Christ. Moreover, he feels strongly that God opened this new door because Cal quit trying to pry the door off the hinges himself. The old career-oriented Cal had. But the new Cal showed reoriented priorities.

Yes, he desired a chance to again be in the mainstream media; but more than that, he desired to always honor God with his lips and work, regardless of his lot.

This attitude is worth highlighting. No matter how much we are convinced that God wants us to succeed in culture and media-shaping vocations, we always need to keep our priorities properly ordered, as Cal learned to do. We do not merely seek success and excellence in our work for our own glory. We are not lambs among wolves for our own benefit. Our goal is not to make ourselves famous, but to make our God famous! Keeping that in mind, God will always bless our efforts. That is what he did with Cal. "It was clearly the blessing of the Lord. He opened the door and nobody could have done that."

That was ten years ago. Suddenly Cal's voice was read in 360 papers in all fifty states. His columns pulled no punches and filled a deep need among readers for a Christ-oriented opinion about major news stories. They still do. Many papers tell him that his column generates more letters—pro and con—than all their other columnists combined. He takes a shot at any target that needs hitting. He does not back off. His words are so tightly knit, his reasoning so well documented, that his opinions ring with truth. For instance, in a November 2, 1993, column, he addressed the matter of bigotry:

> When anyone makes a slur or perceived slander of any group or individual on the politically correct list of protected species, they are roundly denounced in editorials and by spokespersons for the offended class until they are forced to repent in public. ... But there seems to be one class of citizens upon whom it is always open season. You can say anything you like about evangelical Christians and never fear the wrath of the media or the political establishment.

In another 1994 column, Cal highlighted the results of a poll by CBS and the *New York Times* that indicated that evangelical Christians are much more "normal" than major media thought. "Glory be!" writes Cal:

That ought to cause great concern among people who thought they had these folks isolated. Why, employees of the *Times* or CBS might be living closer to one or more of these people than they think. ... The poll ... found the education backgrounds of these people are roughly the same as all Americans! This, after years of portraying conservative Christians as snake handlers, book burners, misogynists, and racists who didn't graduate from real universities and who never read books other than the King James version of the Bible. It is like discovering that blacks are fully human or that women can succeed working outside as well as inside the home. The press continues to flaunt its deliberate ignorance of religion and religious people. Editors would never allow any other group to be portrayed in this manner, especially a group so large.

That is Cal Thomas, lamb among wolves, at his best. Some may not appreciate Cal's very direct and sometimes sarcastic delivery, but I find it refreshing and energizing. And we need him there swinging from the heels, making his (our) points. We need many more like him. Can you be one of them?

It is important to point out that while Cal is straight-ahead with the facts and uses his ready wit to great effect, he is always unfailingly good-humored and courteous. This is perhaps particularly true when he is going head-to-head with those of a "different philosophical base." It was a real blessing to watch him on one of his early television talk shows when his guest was former senator and presidential candidate, George McGovern, a staunch and doctrinaire liberal. Cal's kind demeanor and friendliness were more impressive to me than his cogent questions and sparkling repartee. Cal is a great example for all who would represent Jesus in culture. The people whose philosophies and actions we oppose are not our enemies. They are the reason we are out there. Our goal is not to bash them, it is to help them see a better way—the best way, the only way, the way of Jesus.

Cal's opinions have become valued by Ted Koppel, who has invited Cal to appear on *Nightline* several times. Ted has used him as a consultant for a Memphis-based town meeting on the topic of the Christian right. It is good to know that *Nightline* sought input from a solid Christian thinker.

And in May 1994, Cal received another surprise. Roger Ailes, head of CNBC, was assembling his TV talk-show lineup and called Cal. "I want an openly conservative person on here," he told Cal. He wanted someone to offer a balance to more liberal hosts such as Phil Donahue and Geraldo. But the person needed to be a sane voice who could do more than throw darts at the president. Cal explained to him that there was much more to talk about than President Clinton, though he would not steer clear of legitimate discussions of him. "You're hired," Ailes said. That was that. Today, Cal hosts his own prime-time talk show on Tuesday nights on CNBC. He also hosts his own national radio talk show on Saturday night. "People ask me now, 'Where do you want to be in five years?'" says Cal. "I used to have these kinds of plans, but they never worked out. Now I let God work. He does a much better job of it."

Today Cal and his wife once again live in the suburbs of Washington. On any given Saturday afternoon, you might find him on his cordless phone, out in his yard, planning that night's radio show or granting another interview to this or that major media outlet. He is on top of the media world, a Christian very much in demand for his outspoken, yet thoughtful opinions. He is constantly rubbing shoulders with unbelievers. "Most people now know that I am a believer and most are interested. They don't know many people who are both believers and thoughtful people." This statement tells us a great deal about the need for roaring lambs to be out there among the wolves. Our best, most thoughtful people are desperately needed to be out there in culture, positively telling and showing who Jesus is and why he came.

Cal says that as a Christian, "unbelievers are really the only kind of people worth knowing. Most of my friends are pagans," he says with refreshing candor. Often you will find the Thomas's friends visiting their home for coffee and dessert. Before their invited guests arrive, Cal and his wife pray: "Lord, if you want us to verbally talk about you, then you bring up the opportunity." Then they welcome their guests and have tea and cake and "discussions," says Cal. "We just have conversations." At this point in Cal's career, he is smart enough to know that God can turn the conversation in an instant, whether it is held in an L.A. restaurant or at his home. When the conversation does turn, Cal has the same peace that he found with the two *Times* editors and has no doubt as to what to say: He tells his friends about Jesus.

Terry Mattingly

About as far as is psychologically possible from Cal Thomas's inside-the-beltway haunts are the east Tennessee mountains where Terry Mattingly lives, teaches, and writes. Even if Terry were not a very key lamb, I would still visit him in his secluded corner of the world. As almost any Texan will understand, the trip to Terry's is worth it because he knows barbecue and has access to some of the best produce in the hills and hollers of that very special area. His more casual visitors are taken to an excellent barbecue right there in the small city of Johnson City, Tennessee. However, if you make the trip, do not settle for that. Entreat, cajole, even whine if you have to until Terry takes you out to a spot so obscure that even he might miss the turnoff a time or two before zeroing in on the very best version of Tennessee barbecue extant. Wow! It is great.

Although in a geographic backwater, Terry Mattingly is about as tuned in and connected as anyone I know. He is a master of the

fax machine and E-mail and can cruise the Internet. His computer-
ized Rolodex is legendary, and he can be and often is in contact with
newsmakers of all sorts—particularly if they have any relationship
at all to religion. Terry Mattingly is in on the action.

In fact, he is in the vanguard of action on two important and
crucial fronts. He teaches some of the finest potential roaring lambs
as a professor of communications at Milligan College, and he wades
out into the deep water every week as the nationally syndicated religion columnist for Scripps Howard.

As a faculty member at Milligan, which is a member of the
Coalition for Christian Colleges and Universities, Terry has an
opportunity to have an impact on communications courses across
the whole spectrum of Christian colleges. These programs are currently woefully weak, producing few roaring lambs. The primary
reason, besides limited vision, is the lack of qualified Christian faculty with real hard newsroom experience. This is what makes Terry
such a key and valued player: a solid commitment to serve Jesus
coupled with solid news experience.

After graduating from Baylor University, Terry piled up experience and byline credits as a religion reporter for the *Charlotte News*,
the *Charlotte Observer,* and the *Rocky Mountain News*, a few of the
nation's most respected newspapers, before landing the influential
Scripps Howard weekly syndicated column. For Christian young
people who would like to follow in his footsteps, he has some valu-
able advice.

The first bit of advice may seem obvious. You have to be able to
get a job. Terry says too many Christians think they ought to be able
to hop right onto a religion writing shift. Not so. Most often, you have
to be willing to pay your dues until you get to a point where you have
more control over what and how you write. You get to this point by
writing letters and letters and reporting more and more competently.
Again, excellence is a factor. Personally, Terry thinks that many Christians have a wrong idea about how they might best impact secular jour-

nalism. "They look at the secular press and they see bias against Christians. But they want to replace the bias of secular media with the bias of Christianity. And that's not a viable approach."

What *is* the best way Christians can be salt in secular journalism? Terry says it is being the fairest, most competent reporter in the newsroom. And being highly competent can be harder then being bombastic about your faith. It takes time, effort, and sacrifice. But the payoffs—those times when God suddenly gives the Christian journalist a chance to be salt—are sure to come, though in the tough world of journalism they are likely to come with a few lumps.

In an article written for the *Quill*, a journalism journal, Terry recalls one incident.

"Mattingly," the editor said, "there's too much Jesus in this story."

"It was hard to tell if he was joking. I took him seriously and tried to explain that whenever the person I was writing about opened his mouth, some kind of faith-soaked religious language came out. His speaking style was part of the story, I argued."

The editor was still a little uncomfortable: "Well, okay. Just try to tone it down a little. Okay?"

Terry's tenure at that newspaper and his competent skillful understanding of his craft helped him persuade a crusty editor not to cut Jesus unnecessarily out of an article; that just because the word in question was *Jesus* does not mean that it doesn't have merit if it reflects the person being written about. Do you see why we need more Terry Mattinglys both out there among the wolves and teaching the lambs who should be going out there?

There was another occasion like the one mentioned above while Terry was at the *Rocky Mountain News*, one of Denver's two leading dailies. He recalls in a *Quill* cover story:

> Deadline was three hours away and the *Rocky Mountain News* was bracing for a new wave of abortion protests.
>
> I raised a style question while working on a religion-angle (abortion) story. "Why is it," I asked an assistant city editor, "that we

call one camp *pro-choice*, its chosen label, while we call the other [camp] *anti-abortion*, a term it abhors?"

Nearby, the city editor began listening. "We could," I said, "try to use more neutral terms." I wasn't fond of *anti-abortion*. It seemed to fit Jesse Helms and not Mother Teresa. But it was literal. I suggested a phrase such as *pro-abortion rights*. This might be wordy but would help avoid the editorial spin of *pro-choice*.

The assistant editor said *pro-choice* was accurate, because the real issue was choice, not abortion. In that case, I said, we should be evenhanded and use *pro-life*.

The city editor stepped in. Minus a few descriptive words, here is what he said: Look, the pro-choice people are pro-choice. The people who say they are pro-life aren't really pro-life. They're nothing but a bunch of hypocritical right-wing religious fanatics and we'll call them whatever we want to call them.

That settled that.

That is the world a Christian faces in secular journalism. That is life among the wolves. That is the battle—one of dangerous ideas afloat in the media workrooms, where thoughtful Christians are often outnumbered by the hundreds. Putting your ideas forth can cost you dearly. Remember, no one said that it would be easy.

In fact, Terry's gentle-but-tough stand on the matter of abortion rhetoric—an issue that affects how thousands of readers will perceive groups and their causes—almost cost him his job. Several newsroom staff members tried to bring charges against him for conflict of interest. They tried to have him removed from any coverage of abortion. He asked one of the women if she thought his reporting was biased. She said, "Terry, the vehemence with which you argue for fair coverage of both sides is a sign you are biased."

There it is. Plain and simple. A group that was obviously pro-abortion in their views tried to oust Terry on charges that because he was pro-life, he could not fairly cover the local abortion protests.

Because he wanted *both* sides to be treated fairly, it obviously meant he was biased. What!?

How would you handle a crisis like this? As a believer, what would your response be? I am happy to say that Terry handled it like the champ he is. He saw clearly that the only thing that really mattered—the only place where the playing field was actually level between him and the others—was on this issue: Was his reporting competent and fair or not? Anticipating that something of this sort might come up during the abortion coverage, Terry actually had written his editor a note months earlier. In it, he urged the editors to consider a team approach to reporting the abortion protest, so as to insure that the overall coverage would be fair. That paid off. His editor knew all along that Terry was acting honorably and fairly. This perception and this *reality* is a must for lambs among wolves.

Looking back on that and other war stories from fellow Christian journalists, Terry argues that these days Christians in secular journalism may be some of the last reporters and editors to *really* want to see fair coverage of the issues. This is why we need to be producing more of them.

Today, Terry's journalism as a columnist is of a different brand. "I am encouraged to be unbalanced," he says. When he left the *Rocky Mountain News* to begin teaching communications, he did so with such a good reputation among the editors at Scripps Howard's Washington office that they urged him to continue writing his weekly religion column, which he had begun while at the newspaper.

These days Terry writes on whatever he wants, just about however he wants. He *earned* the right to do so. He has tackled the issue of homosexuality in the Episcopal church. He uses his column to promote positive values. He writes about people such as Ken Wales, helping to promote *Christy* among TV viewers. And he often takes on the issue of religious bias in the secular media. With a master of arts in church-state studies from Baylor and a master of science in journalism from the University of Illinois, Terry has become a sought-after expert in the study and analysis of religion in the media and culture.

His Washington, D.C., Scripps Howard editor once called him a "funky conservative" Christian. "He knows I am a conservative, but he finds it very hard to figure out what I will write about," Terry says. That is because Terry has his finger on the pulse of so many matters. He understands and deciphers cultural trends in movies and TV, reads deep books, and can talk transubstantiation or transcendentalism. In fact, if you throw premillenialism in there he does not blink. He reads Quentin Schultze and Billy Graham.

Terry knows he needs a broad understanding of culture and all faiths to help him be as effective as possible for Christ. He does what it takes to be the best at what he does. Of course, it helps that he is impassioned about the world of words and ideas. But as Terry produces yet another column for his several hundred subscribing newspapers, talking about a world-class classical guitarist who is an outspoken Christian or the emergence of religious books at the Moscow Book Fair, his success can all be traced back to a conscious decision made in the mid-1970s by an eager student who saw a need for Christians to be salt in secular journalism. Recalls Terry of the day it all dawned on him: "I just said, okay, I'm going to be a religion writer!"

Perhaps you can see why I am pleased that Terry Mattingly uses *Roaring Lambs* as a text in one of his courses at Milligan, and why I would continue to make my way to visit with him—even if there were no barbecue.

Fred Barnes

The room was filled with a sampling of the most important people in America—political pundits, inbred intellectuals, and jackal journalists. Hot, white spotlights shone everywhere. Onstage, presidential candidates Walter Mondale and Ronald Reagan stood behind their respective podiums. The air hummed, and adrenaline flowed. Then the moderator turned to three select questioners from the national press. He asked Fred Barnes, political correspondent for the *Baltimore Sun*, to pose a question. Fred, a University of Virginia graduate, who is always dapperly dressed in a way that we tubby Texans can only dream about, looked at the candidates through horn-rimmed glasses and on national television asked both men: "Do you consider yourself a born-again Christian, and what role does your faith play in your decision making?"

Boom!! A shot rang around the nation. In living rooms all over America average folks sat up and took note. Many were too stunned to applaud, though that was surely their second reflex. By contrast, immediately after Fred's question, the room full of stuffy, debate spectators behind him let out a finely tuned hiss. A Washington, D.C., journalist had just done the unthinkable. On a nationally televised presidential debate, Fred Barnes had mentioned the *C* word. Fred dared the two men vying for leadership of the greatest country in the world to say whether, in fact, they were Christians—something they had both claimed to be in smaller, less publicized settings. Fred just wanted it on the record nationally. Further, he dared ask what their faith really meant in their day-to-day life and decision-making processes. Was that unreasonable? When you are a lamb among wolves, many will think it is.

While many average Americans cheered his question, Fred caught flak from fellow Beltway journalists. In the next few days he got piles of mail, mostly from people who were hostile to the idea of Christianity's ever being mentioned in public. Had Fred, graduate of a prestigious university and boy-wonder writer, just sounded the death knell on a bright, promising career? When he returned to Washington from the debate, the phones were ringing. All the talk shows wanted him as a guest.

"I went on every one of them," Fred recalls. And when he did, he issued a stellar, logical defense about why he asked Mondale and Reagan what he did. As a journalist, he said, you ask about what you are interested in. Some ask about foreign policy; some ask about the deficit; Fred asked about the candidates' faith. Four years before the 1984 Reagan-Mondale debates, Fred had accepted Christ. At the time of the debates, he was an evangelical whose work was journalism, and his beat was the White House. So, it seemed only natural to ask the candidates to clear up the untidy statements they had previously made about their faith.

One of the shows on which Fred appeared after the debate was *The McLaughlin Group*, led by former Jesuit priest John McLaughlin. Fred performed well. "When I was on that first time, I waited to be called on, and, as a result, hardly got a word in!" But in the ensuing months, he was asked back to be a guest member of McLaughlin's combative panel, and six years ago he became a regular member of the show, which is one of the most watched of all the Washington talk shows. Not long after his debate bombshell, Fred also was asked, in 1985, to come on board a venerable Washington political journal, the *New Republic*, to write a column about the White House. He recently started a new political magazine, *The Standard*.

Instead of pounding the last nail in his coffin, Fred's national but faithful commitment to his beliefs helped catapult him into national celebrity status. The talk-show appearances ushered Fred into a whole new element of his journalism career.

Please do not get the wrong idea. Fred Barnes is a consummate political columnist. Being a Christian and a Washington watcher does not mean that he is out there every day eyeing the White House to see if the president is having a morning quiet time or not. In fact, the vast majority of what Fred writes would have nothing to do with Christianity in any but the eyes of the most spiritually sensitive and astute observer. It is nitty-gritty, behind-the-scenes journalism about people and their political ideas. To pull this off, he must keep the best, highest-level sources in the best, highest-level places. He must write with a razor sharp pen. His analysis and observations do not just bark, they often have bite to them as well. For all these reasons, Fred is very good—some would say the best—at what he does, and at this point many people know that Fred also happens to be a Christian. When they see Fred, they associate excellence at journalism's highest levels with someone who sincerely follows God. In fact, in an interview in Billy Graham's *Decision* magazine, Fred even credited his conversion with improving his work. "I found that being a Christian made me a better journalist, not a worse one. I discovered I had a greater capacity and more capability for my work. I would write better and faster. God transformed my work habits and then opened up an unimaginable number of journalistic opportunities for me."

Being a believer has also meant that Fred remains sensitive to the issues of faith that other Washington journalists would surely miss. Interestingly, as President Clinton consistently speaks about his faith life and courts evangelical leaders, the rest of the Washington media is starting to come around to appreciating Fred's observations. "The media hasn't gotten attuned to this idea until very recently. That is the notion that your faith does have and should have a tremendously strong bearing on how you carry out your life, whether it is your public life or private life. It's going to affect your leadership. It's going to affect the policies you adopt. Because it is what creates your values. . . . It's really been only recently because of a lot of things that have been written and a lot of work that has been done and a lot of activity by Christians—both political and intellectual activity—that the notion that your religious faith is a legitimate part, a legitimate underpinning for everything you do in politics and public policy. That idea has really only caught on recently and ironically President Clinton has had a lot to do with it, as has Stephen Carter's book, *The Culture of Disbelief*."

The fact that Fred can rightly make this observation and say so publicly is among the strongest indictments of evangelical Christians. We have failed to show through living fully integrated lives that Jesus does, in fact, relate to our calling in life and should have a tremendous influence on the way we live every part.

Every Thursday at 11:00 A.M., the editors of the *New Republic*, long known for establishing much of what is considered conventional political wisdom in Washington, gather around a long conference table to talk about story ideas. One person pitches an idea and others take their swings at it. In the room are gathered a homosexual Roman Catholic, several secular Jews, and other journalists who have little or no faith life. Nonetheless, several remain open to exploring the role of religion in politics. Again, we Christians usually are not shut out. Most often, we have had no one there to enter in. That is our fault. We can be very thankful we have had Fred at the *New Republic*.

During the 1992 presidential campaign, Fred visited Notre Dame. He had heard about Clinton's recent campaign visit there, and the way the candidate had frankly spoken of his faith. Fred went back to one of the magazine's editorial meetings and pitched an idea to his fellow journalists. What about doing a story on Clinton's claims of Christian faith and how he skillfully uses them as a political tool? Before the editorial meeting was over, Fred had made his point and had sold the idea. Moreover, he had won the support of his publisher, a secular Jew. So he wrote the story, one of the first to highlight Clinton's use of Christianity as a political tool. Since then, Fred has devoted several columns to now-President Clinton's cunning courting of moderate evangelicals. Again, says Fred, "I write about what I am interested in." In one column, Fred's writing took an interesting side road. While documenting a visit that one group of evangelicals had with the president, Fred noted how many of these evangelicals had been "softened" toward Clinton because of his skillful courting. "What's amazing is Clinton's skill in playing down moral differences he has with these evangelicals, such as his support of abortion and gay rights."

This insight provided material for one of Fred's classic columns in which he used his considerable journalistic skills not only to chide the president over moral issues, but also to take a feathery but instructive swipe at his fellow evangelicals for minimizing differences on matters of extreme moral importance to committed Christians. Of course, Fred's views are just that—his own and no one else's. But they are sharp and cogent. And most importantly, they've gone out to thousands of important readers of all ilks and creeds via the *New Republic*. Fred is being salt, not only to an unbelieving public, but also to his fellow believers!

Fred stands for Christian principles in a very key spot. When the magazine's editorial staff recently caught Washington's fervor to criticize the once-again rising influence of Christians in politics via the Christian Coalition, Fred was a voice of reason. While the stories about the religious right that emerged from those editorial meetings still were not completely to his liking, he nonetheless was able to "salt" the talk. The stories, while critical, never became disrespectful of religious faith.

But Fred's work far exceeds print journalism these days. He probably gets his most frequent and best chances to speak for moral values and religious faith during those electric sagas taped every Friday evening called *The McLaughlin Group*. Fred uses the brief drive between his magazine's office and northwest Washington for prayer. "I do that all the time. . . . *The McLaughlin Group* is a funny kind of show. You want to do the best you can. You want to be knowledgeable, but you also want to be the kind of person the Lord wants you to be." That can be hard sometimes when four other people are yelling to be heard about some foreign policy point—the winner gets all the camera attention.

Fred pulls up adjacent to National Presbyterian Church and the campus of the American University. He walks into a building and emerges onto the show's set. Three . . . Two . . . One. They are on. Five mouths move in semisyncopated fashion, led by the bulldoggish but loving, baton-wielding show host John McLaughlin. It is improvisational, political commentary at its finest, and thousands of viewers tune in.

What do they see? Well, in this largely unedited forum, some-times the discussion turns to the inner city and its plight. On Fred's right sits a rotund, bearlike man named Jack Germond, the epitome of a crusty newspaperman. He is an atheist, a smoker, a heavy drinker, and a liberal's liberal. More money, better funding for this or that government program, is Jack's often-heard rhetoric.

"What about you, Freddie Beetle Barnes?" McLaughlin asks, whipping the talk and the cameras Fred's way and referring to him affectionately by his personalized nickname.

The director zooms in on Barnes; audio is up; ears open around the country. "Here's a case," Fred might say, as he has in one form or fashion on several occasions during the show, "where I believe no government program is going to change the inner city; it's going to be religious faith that's going to do it."

At this point, Jack is likely to chuckle under his breath. Fred continues: "And that's the only thing that is going to do it. You can't just go and train people. You have to give them the power to over-come." Fred draws an analogy between America in the 1980s and 1990s and historic England. The cities of America today face chal-lenges similar to the cities of England in the early eighteenth cen-tury after gin was invented. There had been a huge influx of people into London, and there was a burgeoning class with all the social pathologies we now see of addiction, murder, abuse, broken fami-lies, and so on. One person in particular had a tremendous impact in changing that England, but that was not anybody in Parliament. It was John Wesley, who had the right advice to men: stop drinking, stay with your families, go to work. But the important thing was that he gave them the power to do that. Advice was not enough. He had to give them Jesus Christ and faith in Jesus because that would empower them to live the kind of lives that they should lead, lives that would try to approach purity. They could not do it otherwise; it had to be faith. It was religious faith that transformed the cities of England and had so much to do with wiping out this poor underclass.

"About this time, Germond is probably sneering. I just know that is coming," Fred says of such encounters, "but Jack and I are friends. He was my boss at the *Washington Star* newspaper. I know he thinks religion is bunk." This little episode says so much about what it means to be an effective lamb among the wolves of the world, wolves Jesus also dearly loves.

Across the table catercorner to Fred sits Mort Kondrake. Mort was also formerly with the *New Republic*. He is Fred's best friend. By Fred's own description, Mort is a searcher. In recent years, Mort, himself an extremely persuasive writer and speaker, has found something—really some*one*. His name is Jesus. Fred Barnes' life and example helped bring about the introduction. This is another example of the influence Fred has in Washington. It is off the set and off the printed page; it is relational, real, and regular.

About a year ago, some influential Washington men were starting a monthly Bible study. Among those who would be gathering for fellowship, encouragement, and regular Bible study were several top area businessmen, a clergyman from Fred's church, a member of a leading think tank, and Fred, the journalist. Fred told his wife Barbara about the new group. "That is perfect for Mort," she said. Fred agreed and invited him to be a part of the gathering. Today, the group meets monthly, high up in a Watergate building. They sit around a marble conference table that looks out over the Potomac River and share battle stories—"our blessings and our anxieties," says Fred.

And there *are* both blessings and anxieties. This is part of being a lamb among wolves. It is not always easy, and the lambs do not win every skirmish—especially in a town like Washington, which is built on ideas and the words that frame them. In a town like that, the apostle James' admonition to watch your tongue is probably some of the best advice possible. As a Christian, Fred must be all the more sensitive.

He tells of an incident on *Nightline* when, in the give-and-take of live television, he criticized a reporter's story, which he had not actually read. What is more, the reporter knew he had not read it. Later, in a letter, the reporter let Fred know what a jerk he had been to do that. Fred's response was an admission that he had been wrong and an appeal for forgiveness. Christians do not always get it right the first time, but when we apologize and ask forgiveness, we usually make a friend. Fred did in this case. The reporter was so overwhelmed that a journalist of Fred's stature would apologize that he could hardly believe it and graciously granted Fred forgiveness. Score one for the lambs.

✳

Obviously, we need more people like Jim Russell, Cal Thomas, Terry Mattingly, and Fred Barnes. As one who has great interest in our Christian colleges, it is striking to note the absence of graduates in key journalistic roles. All of us must help our schools do a better job in this area. Too, our churches must point talented young people toward this area of service. As a start, every church should have a Church Writing Group. Beyond that, churches need to have Christian journalism conferences in the same way that they have missionary conferences. Christian journalists should be brought in to help young people find clear paths into a career of journalism and service in God's kingdom. Above all, we should show support for all those who choose this career path by praying for them and by letting their publications know that we appreciate them.

4

Lambs and the Movies: Silver Screens

It is tough for anyone to break into the movies. It is particularly tough for Christians, for two reasons. First, we do not have key Christians in place in the movie business. Most reins of power are held by those who, if not hostile to Christians, are oblivious to them. Some Christians who are in the movie business believe that there is so much hostility that they must keep their faith a secret in order to work. Second, movies are very expensive to produce. A relatively modest Hollywood production can easily run to eight figures. Even more daunting is the fact that after you have your multimillion-dollar movie produced, you have to distribute it in order not only for people to see it but also to have any chance of recouping your investment. Distribution channels are so tightly controlled and the ways of doing business so arcane that the chance for an "outsider," or independent movie, no matter how good, to gain access to quality distribution is the ultimate long shot.

Having said this, I believe that Christians must be in the movies. We have no choice if we are to be obedient. Movies and the movie business may be our "uttermost parts," but we are commanded to go there. The movie business may be daunting; the Hollywood environment may be hostile, but is taking on the movie business too difficult for committed Christians armed with the Holy Spirit? Is the movie industry too tough for God? The answer is obviously no. The reason that Christians are not in the movie business is because we have not thought strategically and have not exercised faith. We need to begin doing both.

When the movie business begins to look like it is too big to tackle, think of the country of China when missionary James Hudson Taylor first went there. Or think of Africa when missionary David Livingstone went there. Both China and Africa are huge and complex. Hollywood and the whole movie industry are minuscule and simple by comparison. Think of the great victories that God has given when people of faith such as Taylor and Livingstone have stepped out on his promises. Then think about being a roaring lamb among the wolves of Hollywood. Still not easy, but eminently doable with prayer, commitment, and reliance on the Holy Spirit.

To encourage you further, meet four people who are there, who are taking Hollywood head-on—being obedient, surviving, and even prospering as lambs among wolves. Readers of *Roaring Lambs* will have already met Frank Schroeder, but in this book you will get to know him and his work better and more fully.

Frank Schroeder

Before film critic Michael Medved burst Hollywood's R-rated balloon in 1992 with the release of his book, *Hollywood Vs. America: Popular Culture and the War on Traditional Values*, Frank had already pricked the film industry's bubble. The forty-year-old filmmaker is a talented self-starter. In his still-young career, the energetic Louisianan has broken fresh ground in Hollywood on more than one occasion, catching the attention of both the establishment and the bankrollers.

One August day in 1991, a tirelessly determined Frank picked up a copy of the *Hollywood Reporter*, the inside-the-industry publication for the movie business, and read: "Frank Schroeder Creates a Market for G-rated Films." The Baton Rouge boy's creative thinking and commitment to making and marketing wholesome, excellent family films was "raising eyebrows in the industry," the *Reporter* said. I had picked up a copy of that same edition of the *Reporter*, and it certainly raised *my* eyebrows. I determined then to get to know Frank Schroeder.

Would you also like to "raise some eyebrows" in Hollywood? To do so will take some of the drive, commitment, and vision of a Frank Schroeder. It will mean walking by faith instead of by sight. But if you like the exhilaration of a roller-coaster ride coupled with the joy of being obedient to the command to be salt, it may be the trip for you.

Fresh out of LSU in 1979 and Regent University in 1981 with a master's degree in communications, Frank was immediately in demand as a consultant to many Christian television ministries. But, as he went about his work, one thing became very clear: Those groups were "preaching to the choir." So he started doing some of his own research. He found that the ministries for whom he was consulting were only reaching about 4 to 6 percent of the country with the Gospel message.

Frank thought back to the model of communication that he had learned at Regent. It was the pattern that Jesus himself had set. First, Jesus engaged in mass communication, though in parables; second, Jesus engaged in group communications of about twelve to fifty people; and finally, he engaged in one-on-one communication. Frank found one thing to be clear: The mass communication that most Christian ministries were doing was not parable or story. It was in-your-face didacticism. Where were the good stories with the Christian message?

About this same time, Frank met with a man who had a sports background and who shared the same vision. As they talked, an idea emerged for something truly unique—a mainstream sports television talk show hosted by a major Christian sports figure whose guests would be Christians too. Frank's friend promised to back the show financially if he would produce it. What emerged was a groundbreaking sports talk show hosted by committed Christian and all-everything basketball player, Julius Erving. *Julius Erving's*

Sports Focus gave people a peek at the top players they admired. Schroeder and Erving took their viewers into the athlete's life, sketching a video picture of the player's whole person, not just his or her sports persona. For instance, people saw Walter Payton as a family man and committed believer. A whole new forum was suddenly open to reach people in a professional and interactive way with the Gospel. "The athletes' lights were shining, but not in a preachy format," says Frank, "and it was reaching guys who were drinking beer on a Saturday afternoon at the local bar."

Julius Erving's Sports Focus ran for two years. The Christian financial and business community, however, did not step up and rally around and invest advertising and promotional dollars to back a quality effort, and what happens to many quality creative efforts by Christians happened to this show. Frank and his partner were pretty much on their own and, after awhile, they wore down.

Earlier, though, while shooting an interview segment for the show, Frank had sat mesmerized. The guy being profiled was very special, possessing amazing charisma and an even more amazing life story. "Pistol" Pete Maravich was his name, and his brand of basketball, honed at LSU and displayed for years in the pros, had helped change the game. "The Pistol" had introduced flashy elements to the game, including behind-the-back passes and long-range jump shots. Frank had grown up just down the road from LSU and had watched with awe as the Pistol performed his court magic. Now they were in the same room. Afterward, Frank approached Maravich. "Your life story would make a great movie," he said. "Would you be interested in having someone make a film about you?" Maravich said he would pray about it.

In the meantime, Frank and writer Darrel Campbell collaborated with Maravich on his biography, *Heir to a Dream*, which became a Christian best-seller. They eventually began a four-year project to produce a movie about Maravich's eighth-grade year, which was the story Pete wanted to tell. His eighth-grade year was the basis of his starting position on his championship varsity team. It was the basis of his relationship with his father, "Press," who coached him in high school and at LSU. It was also the basis of his rapid rise to national fame.

In 1989, just two months after the book was finished and in the middle of casting the movie, Pete died at age forty while playing a pickup game of basketball. Suddenly, every film producer in Hollywood wanted Maravich's story. But they wanted a story about Maravich's whole life, against Pete's personal wishes to highlight only his eighth-grade year.

"This is what his last request was," Frank kept telling executives. "It's what he was doing when he died, and we're going to honor a dying man's last wish." The Hollywood execs said their usual thanks but no thanks. Frank and his partners were now on their own, lambs among wolves, carrying out the vision Pete had for a film about strong family relationships. They worked hard and produced a truly exciting, uplifting film: *The Pistol: The Birth of a Legend.*

But no commercial distributor would take the film. They test-marketed the movie in three midsize Southern cities and it did gangbusters. Still Frank kept getting the same answer: "Your film is too soft"; translation: Your film is rated G.

How long would *you* last after constantly getting those kinds of replies? Frank kept going. He took the film around to many film shows, like one in Las Vegas where three hundred companies were showing their new productions at a big hotel entertainment center. Frank recalls entertaining a group of Japanese buyers in his suite (every producer has a suite where they offer food and snippets of their film on video. Non-Christian producers sometimes offer a lot more.) The Japanese buyers were watching *The Pistol* with interest. They turned to Frank: "We don't like basketball in Japan. We're very short in Japan. We cannot sell basketball in our country." *Oh, well,* Frank thought. "But we *can* sell family," they added. Boom! Frank had his first sale. The group distributed the film to seventy companies worldwide.

Getting an American distributor was still proving to be futile. Yet Frank did not stop; instead, he got creative. The former marketer came up with a novel idea: Seek a corporate sponsor to fund distribution of the movie in exchange for an on-screen commercial. The idea seemed to be a winner. It took a year and a half, however, to find a sponsor who would agree. Frank pitched the idea to fifty-five different corporations. Finally, the Chick-fil-A chain came on board. (I am still buying Chick-fil-A sandwiches, both because they are very good and because I admire this Christian-led company that stepped up to a soundly created business opportunity.)

Still, there was one more hurdle to clear. Frank had to convince a cinema chain that running his movie with Chick-fil-A as a sponsor was a good bet. Most of the top chains flatly refused to even consider it. Again, Frank did not stop. "At least watch the film first," Frank advised the executives from General Cinema, the third largest circuit in America. They agreed, and when they saw it, they voted yes. Three other cinema chains followed suit. Frank had broken through at last.

The Pistol was hitting from long range now. If you had gone to see *The Pistol* at one of the nearly forty screens it originally opened on, you would have first been greeted on-screen by Chick-fil-A founder and chairman, S. Truett Cathy, who expressed concern at the changing content of films, mentioned his company's commitment to family values, and invited viewers to enjoy the movie.

The venture paid off. The movie was well-received in its first four months in ninety-one theaters and was eventually released broadly in American markets. If you have the opportunity, I hope you will go see *The Pistol* and buy a Chick-fil-A sandwich. Sony SVS picked up video distribution rights on the film, and that is where Frank says it will earn the most money in the future.

Money is nice; it is the bottom line for many in the industry. For Frank and his partner, cracking the "Hollywood Wall" with G-rated, reality-based films as a way to be obedient to Jesus' admonition to be salt was, and continues to be, the goal. The last time I was with Frank, he was not only full of plans to produce two other films he has in mind to complete a "Pistol trilogy" but was also looking at other possible projects. Frank Schroeder is a hero, a lamb succeeding among some of the toughest wolves anywhere.

John Herklotz

Another of my own personal heroes is John Herklotz, who, like Frank Schroeder, is also going head-to-head with the wolves in Hollywood, and like Frank, is finding the going tough but rewarding. Again, being obedient is not always easy, but it does produce great satisfaction and great joy.

John is a prime example of someone who is determined to make a difference. John has been blessed, and he recognizes his blessings and the responsibilities that accompany them. After serving as chief financial officer of the *Chicago Tribune* from 1951–1961 and as auditor and controller for WGN Continental Broadcasting from 1961–1968, John eventually hit it very big when he won the rural cellular telephone license in New Mexico. Years later, in 1990, he made millions when he sold his cellular company to Centel Corporation.

Since then, John has looked for ways to wisely invest and donate his money to make a positive, value-laden difference. Paul describes John's spiritual gift in Romans 12:8: "…if it is contributing to the needs of others, let him give generously." John is living out this Scripture. Christian colleges, God-glorifying art endeavors, and student-citizenship projects are only some of the causes to which he contributes. But there is another way in which John Herklotz is putting his resources to work, and it is the one on which we want to focus.

In the mid-1980s, when family films seemed almost nonexistent, John attended a National Religious Broadcasters convention where he met Richard Kiel. Richard is the massive man who played Jaws to Roger Moore's James Bond in *The Spy Who Loved Me* and *Moonraker*, as well as playing a host of successful roles in other movies including *Silver Streak* and *Cannonball Run 2*. As the two men visited, Richard shared with John his dream to produce *The Giant of Thunder Mountain*, a screenplay he had written.

John became excited for several reasons. One, it was a clean, G-rated screenplay that the whole family could watch. Two, it included wonderful scenery from Yosemite National Park, where it was eventually filmed. But more than that, its message was universal and Christian: Don't judge a book by its cover. John explains, "You can't judge a person or a situation just by outward appearances. Richard Kiel really had the idea. It relates to his life as a literal giant." In fact, Richard's life has been one of sticking out in a crowd. He had dealt for years with the pain of being different—of being judged simply by outward appearances. The story he wrote communicated how wrong it is to make surface judgments and of the need to see the heart.

John spared no expense in producing *The Giant of Thunder Mountain*. Besides Kiel, John enlisted Jack Elam, star of more than ninety-five feature films (half of which were westerns), and a regular television guest on programs like *Bonanza*, *Gunsmoke*, *Home Improvement*, and many more series, including *Lonesome Dove*. Marianne Rogers, then-wife of singer Kenny Rogers, herself an actress with many credits, also stars in the movie. Foster Brooks, known for his remarkable on-screen depictions of the classic inebriate, and William Sanderson, known for his role as Larry in the hit TV series *Newhart* are featured as well. The narration is done by Academy- and Emmy-Award-winning actress Cloris Leachman. It is no cheap film.

As it turns out, *The Giant of Thunder Mountain* is a wonderful film that the whole family can enjoy. It is one that parents and their children can discuss afterward, and it actually has a positive, value-laden message. I had the great privilege of helping in a very small way when John tested the film in the Dallas market. The test turned out to be a very personal one for me. Our daughter Leigh was visiting with our grandsons. She took Bobby and Todd to see *The Giant of Thunder Mountain.* They loved it (and still watch the video at home). The sophisticated film reviewer of the *Dallas Morning News* hated it. I will take my grandsons' judgment any time.

One great thing about investing in films these days is the home-video aftermarket. *The Giant of Thunder Mountain* will be in the video stores as a legacy to John and his faithfulness for many years. John hopes its message will reach many children, and more importantly, their parents as well. "Movies and TV have a powerful influence on today's youth," he says. "I made *The Giant of Thunder Mountain* to provide an exciting alternative to the violent and exploitive influence on-screen."

John has also founded the Family Films Foundation. It is just another way in which he is seeking to make a positive difference—to be salt and light. "I'd like to see [the foundation] become something to enable or assist others in pursuing their dreams and goals to develop family films." John Herklotz, a roarer, drowns out the wolves.

Darlene Koldenhoven

My friend Dr. Robert Smith, the president of Greenville College, called me and said, "We just had one of your roaring lambs speak in chapel here at the college today." When he told me about her message, her amazing talent, her professional background, and her commitment to Christ, I knew Darlene Koldenhoven was someone I wanted very badly to meet. Since then, she has become a wonderful sister in the faith and continues to inspire me with the courageous use of her talent.

You have probably seen Darlene and not been aware of her identity. You almost surely have heard her. Darlene Koldenhoven is the statuesque, 5'10" blonde who emerges onstage with a five-octave voice, singing like a mythical siren during Greek musician Yanni's much-touted "Live at the Acropolis" concert in Athens, Greece. The

1993 production of the musician's extremely popular compositions is already one of public television's biggest hits ever, being replayed time after time. The *Chicago Tribune*'s rave review of the concert singled out Darlene's performance: "Another highlight was the concert's only vocal performance in which first soprano Darlene Koldenhoven and second soprano Lynn Davis came from the wings singing *Aria*, an operatic duet."

If you have not seen this Grammy Award-winning singer (best Jazz Vocal Performance in 1987 while working with musical genius Clare Fischer) on public television, perhaps you did in an altogether different venue. Darlene was in the sensational choir of singing nuns in *Sister Act* and *Sister Act II*. In fact, Darlene arranged the music and rehearsed the choir into form, taking them from an amateurish to a professional sound much like Whoopie Goldberg's fictitious character does during the movie. When Darlene sang the words to those traditional and modern church songs, she really meant it! Obviously, her enthusiasm for the music and commitment to excellence in preparing the group paid off.

"I found that the songs were so exciting to sing and the whole message was so enthusiastic that people were singing with gusto right from the get-go," she recalls. During their rehearsals and the live shootings, many cast and crew would sit and listen. Several at one point or another told Darlene that the music and lyrics really touched them. They said that if the music at church was really like that, they would be there in a flash!

Let me ask you: Who else could have penetrated a Hollywood motion-picture set, composed of people ranging from atheists to New Age to church burnouts? Do you think that many of them ever planned on dropping by the local First Baptist's Sunday morning service? It is doubtful. But Darlene, because of years committed to sharpening and marketing her remarkable talents, and because of her vision for penetrating the heart of Hollywood, brought church to them! Salt! Light! Roooar!

"Of course, it helps to have God working as your manager," notes Darlene. After initially being hired simply to rehearse and arrange the music for *Sister Act*, she was encouraged to try out for one of the actual nun roles. She appeared before the casting directors wearing a habit she had kept from a college theatrical role. They loved her and asked her back for a second tryout. When she came, they gave her the job on the spot, telling her that of the hundreds of people whom they had auditioned across the country for parts in *Sister Act*, she was the only one they had hired on the spot! Who, I ask, is behind that?

When people in the industry ask her how she gets the opportunities she does, Darlene sometime replies: "I've got the best manager in the whole world."

"Who is this guy?" they ask eagerly.

"Well, he's world famous. Sometimes he can be selective about whom he chooses" (a little of Darlene's Reformed theology here).

"Well, would you give me his number?"

"Sure," Darlene replies. "It's 1–800–Jesus!"

The bulk of Darlene's work has been as a studio or background vocalist or vocals coach. Over the years, this Christian Reformed church member has landed noteworthy after noteworthy opportunity. Besides performing in the *Sister Act* movies, *A League of Their Own,* and *What about Bob?* she was a vocal coach during the filming of the highly acclaimed movie, *Tina—What's Love Got To Do With It?* She has sung off camera for *A Muppet Christmas Carol, American Tale II, Dances with Wolves, Fletch Lives!, Free Willy, Home Alone, Home Alone II, Hunt for Red October, The Princess Bride, Sneakers,* and many more movies.

She has performed on the *Arsenio Hall Show*, CNN, *Good Morning America, The Home Show, Murder She Wrote, Sunday Morning with Charles Kuralt, Vicki!,* and many others. And she has sung background vocals for the likes of Peter Cetera, Kenny Loggins, Ray Charles, Ringo Starr, the Carpenters, Bette Midler, and David Byrne.

Impressive? That is the short list! Beyond that, Darlene has done scores of commercials and benefits, including singing for evangelist Luis Palau's crusades and on the "Jerry Lewis Telethon."

Darlene, who grew up in a cloistered Dutch Reformed environment on Chicago's south side, has penetrated Hollywood. A lone, very courageous lamb, it took much effort for her to break out of a church mind-set that encouraged her to play classical and sacred music (she is an accomplished pianist), but held that popular music and movies should be off-limits to Christians. Now she is inside, rubbing shoulders and exchanging ideas with people who really matter in the business. Some believers berate her decision to work on R-rated movies or sing with musicians such as Yanni whose music some call New Age. She understands that. She does politely decline offers she considers unsuitable, such as when Playboy asked her to sing in one of its movies. Even then, she asserts, as Christians we need to be polite and tactful. "I'm sorry," she told the Playboy producer. "I'm really not the right call for this because of my belief system. But thanks for thinking of me, and keep me in mind down the line if you do other projects." Darlene notes that that same producer may be doing a G-rated Disney film next year.

"This business is so word-of-mouth, so socially involved. You never know where your next job will come from."

When she gets assignments to do movies or to sing with secular artists, it often opens a whole world of opportunities for witness. "On breaks," she notes, "you have the chance to sit around and discuss things with coworkers." Hollywood is populated with people who love ideas. It is a massive Aeropagus. There have just not been too many people there sharing the idea of Jesus. Darlene is a Paul in the middle of it. When she takes work on an R-rated movie, she is actually increasing her chances of being among the very people Christians ought to want to reach. "Then you have the opportunity to say, 'This is how I believe. This is what Jesus means to me.'"

Do you think she is kidding? Not long ago, a Jewish composer called her to see if she would sing for one of his projects. It happened that the Christmas holidays were coming up, and their phone conversation turned in that direction. He acknowledged his Jewish heritage. Darlene saw an entrance, and asked enthusiastically, "Are you Orthodox, Conservative, or Reformed?" Then she continued, "What does your religion mean with regard to your personal life and faith?"

Boom! Silence—no answer.

Finally, he replied that he did not really know, and then asked her how her own faith mattered in her daily life. "Well, it's very alive," she enthusiastically replied. "It's what keeps me going from one job to the next." A wonderful door had been opened. Darlene looks forward to following up as the Lord leads. But what if Darlene had decided not to work for Jews?—no opportunity, no salt.

On another occasion, a well-known Jewish filmmaker invited Darlene to be his guest at a screening of a new movie made by some Jews in Hollywood who were promoting positive values. Afterward, the two joined several actors and directors at a posh Beverly Hills restaurant to eat and to discuss the screening. When they sat down, her host introduced her to the group of Hollywood insiders: "This is my friend, Darlene. She is a real Dutch Calvinist!"

Everyone laughed. It was an unusual introduction. But even more startling was one person's reaction: "So what does it mean to be a Dutch Calvinist? We've heard about your type but never really met one."

Wow! Talk about an open-ended question. The person's question is both heartening and sad. Sad in the sense that in all of Hollywood, Darlene is such a rarity that these people had never encountered anyone like her. Their information about Christians, to the extent that they had any, had all been secondhand and probably distorted. And we wonder why movies almost always get it wrong when it comes to portraying Christians or what we believe! But the question was heartening in that, at least this one time, Darlene was there to give these people a quick, attractive answer. For awhile that night, it was the heart of the conversation around the table.

This is what it means to penetrate Hollywood. According to Darlene, it means always being professional and always being your best. Lest somehow you have received the wrong impression up to now, going Darlene's route means tough times, too. In Hollywood you need to be able to take a lot of unkindness. You always have to smile. You have to show immense patience with producers and directors who snap at the slightest thing. And you have to be easily adaptable.

Darlene's trained voice allows her to sing in just about whatever style a composer or producer wants. That means she gets a variety of good assignments, like the one with composer Alan Menken. When he needed somebody to sing the female lead on a demo tape for the song "Beauty and the Beast," he turned to Darlene. The result was that Darlene helped craft one of the most popular modern tunes ever, one that raised the spirits of millions who have heard it in its final rendition sung by Peabo Bryson and Celine Dion. And while the song is not Christian per se, its message positively extols the merits of real love that is not bound by exterior façades but is based on true, inner beauty. Darlene's witness, her "saltiness," comes not only in one-on-one encounters but also in helping fill the airwaves with good, value-laden music.

After working with Darlene, Andy Hill, director of music production at Walt Disney Pictures, said, "It is my job to round up superbly talented individuals who can work together at the high level that Disney demands. Darlene Koldenhoven is certainly one of those talents we hope to draw on again and again." That raises another point. As a Christian and as a professional working with God as her manager, Darlene is someone whose abilities and ethics get her re-invitations. This is vital. As Christians in media, we must be so good and so enjoyable to work with that the word spreads, as it did for Darlene with Disney.

Darlene has now set out on another adventure. Much like Amy Grant and Michael W. Smith, Darlene has recognized the need for high-quality pop songs that are constructive and value positive— songs today's teens can listen to and enjoy without mom and dad worrying. So she has recently written and produced her first album, *Keys to the World*, which is packed with ten pop adult/contemporary songs dealing with everything from a healthy view of love to having good self-esteem. The effort has gotten good reviews from the likes of rock star Peter Gabriel. "I loved your singing," he wrote her. *New York Post* film critic Michael Medved said that the album "displays both intensity and professionalism."

Despite the good reviews, some Christian stations and marketing groups have declined to air her music because it failed what they call the "J-count." That is a phrase used for how many times the name *Jesus* is mentioned in a song! This is shortsighted and counterproductive.

Today Darlene spends a healthy portion of her time touring, performing her music, and often speaking at churches and Christian colleges about the need for Christians to get into the performing arts and be open to working in Hollywood. Ironically, before Darlene ever read my book, *Roaring Lambs*, she had entitled one of her seminars "Lambs in the Lion's Den"! In this seminar she talks about demythologizing Hollywood and about taking on un-Christian, self-righteous attitudes. She gives a glimpse into what being a Christian in the "Biz" is like. She helps people in her seminars discover and develop their talents. And as she tours America, she issues a challenge, calling for "entertainment missionaries," talented people who will catch the vision for "becoming industry leaders, not followers," who, like the biblical Esther, will penetrate their culture for God's appointed task.

She knows what she is facing. In many Christian communities, the word *Hollywood* is almost on a par with the word *hell*. Going to a third-world country to witness for Christ is considered admirable;

going to Hollywood is considered grounds for rebuke. However, in recent years, as Darlene has made presentations to church groups around the country, she has seen some hopeful signs. But the old attitudes still persist. One group struck her name out of the bulletin and canceled her appearance without even really talking to her. They simply heard she was from Hollywood and called her a "New Age heretic."

People like Darlene are always going to get it from both sides. Some in Hollywood will mock her for the mere fact that she dares to follow Jesus. Some of her Christian brothers and sisters prefer to peer though the magnifying glass at each jot and tittle, screaming if a single *i* goes undotted.

There is the tension. Could you handle it? Could you become one of Christ's lambs in Hollywood? Are you ready to go from job to job—even if you are great like Darlene—not always knowing where your next paycheck will come from? If you are like Darlene, you will be able to handle the tensions and tough times because you have a sense of calling, a love for people, a faith that will keep you, and a great Manager!

Laverne Barton

The story of the final movie lamb about whom I want you to know is perhaps the most inspiring and the most instructive. It may also be the most convicting for those of us who are not sensitive to God's calling and who see many reasons why we cannot go out there among the wolves to work for and represent him. While connections, talent, and years of study might certainly help someone pursue a culture-influencing role, what a person needs more than anything else is a driving passion that comes from a God-given vision. I want you to know that, no matter what your station in life, you can start making a difference right now. All that is required is a willing spirit and a strong vision.

Laverne Barton has both. Laverne is a real estate agent, wife, and mother living in suburban Nashville who has embarked on an extraordinary journey of faith to write and produce her own motion picture. The journey started unspectacularly one morning in her suburban home.

As her husband Tom was shaving and getting ready for his workday, something kept bugging him. Finally, he told Laverne that a story he had noticed in the news was haunting him: A Lebanese gunman had invaded a worship service at a Christian orphanage and had fatally shot a male missionary, leaving his wife widowed with more than thirty orphans to feed.

As Tom recounted the story, Laverne's heart was pierced to the core. She felt for the widowed missionary. *What a tremendous injustice*, she thought. Suddenly, Laverne, too, became preoccupied with the event, which had only amounted to a world-news brief in their local Tennessee newspaper.

What about the woman's family? she wondered. "I didn't want them to think they were alone," Laverne says. So she did some research and finally uncovered the name and address of the widowed missionary, Barbara Robinson. Then she wrote her a letter. Shortly after, Laverne received a letter from Barbara. "It has been forty days since Bill was murdered and our God is the same and our calling is the same," Barbara wrote.

Laverne was dumbfounded by the woman's faith, and a three-year exchange of letters ensued. "I saw these people as *extraordinary* people of faith. But one thing Barbara wanted to make clear is that she and her husband were *ordinary* people serving an *extraordinary* God."

The more the two communicated, the more Laverne was impressed by Barbara's story. It exemplified what Christianity is really about—godly sacrifice, real faith, and Christlike forgiveness. Laverne thought the story was so important that it needed to be told to others. So she wrote a church play that was produced by Christ Church in Nashville during its missionary conference. It was a special joy when Barbara, who had not been stateside in more than ten years, was flown in for the big event. As the two women visited in person, Laverne's admiration for this simply dressed woman of deep faith grew even more.

"If I could," Laverne finally told her one day shortly after Barbara had returned to Lebanon, "I would work full-time on getting this story made into a film."

The next day at church, Laverne sensed strongly that she should, in fact, embark on that very mission. Her son and husband offered their support. Shortly after, she met with her senior pastor. "Laverne, I think the Lord has called you to do this," he said. "Now what can I do to help?"

That was her confirmation.

Laverne knew what she was after now: She wanted to tell this story not just to Christian audiences, but to mainstream Americans, people whose view of Christian devotion has often been skewed by belligerent politicians or protesters. "People need to know that there are these kinds of Christians," Laverne says.

In the following weeks, Laverne worked hard to find a professional who would write the script. For various reasons, no one jumped on board. "Laverne, you know you're probably going to have to do this yourself," her pastor finally told her. "And you need to think of this as a marathon, not a sprint."

Laverne quit her job as a real estate agent with the full support of her husband and family, which meant losing extra family income. They all decided it was worth it. The family emptied an extra bedroom in their home and set up an office for Laverne. Sequestered from much of her normal routine, Laverne spent months working on a first draft of the script. Laverne and a close friend and colaborer, former Tennessee state senator Norma Crow have founded a corporation called Potter's Productions that will eventually produce films based on true stories of faith-filled people who conquer obstacles. I was pleased to get a letter from Norma last year indicating that the two had read *Roaring Lambs* and had drawn encouragement from it. Norma wrote to say that they stumbled on *Roaring Lambs* in a bookstore while researching information for Laverne's script. "We both knew this book was for us on Saturday, July 30, 1994, in a Christian bookstore in Nashville, Tennessee," writes Norma. "Your book confirmed what we are doing."

In 1994, the two traveled to Israel in an attempt to enter Lebanon to visit Barbara. Their efforts at gaining lawful passage into Lebanon were thwarted, but they actually happened onto one of Barbara's former orphanage workers who was in Israel at the time. Her input into Laverne's script was invaluable.

Laverne is still polishing the script. In the process, she has read books on Lebanon and about missionaries as well as about countless other subjects. She has studied the art and craft of script writing. Eventually, she will begin seeking a producer and financial backing. Many hurdles lie ahead. But Laverne Barton, flanked by a supportive family, church, wise pastor, and visionary friends like Norma Crow, is in the action. She is not on the sidelines. She is not wringing her hands and wishing. She is in there.

Has she made sacrifices? She has made some, but what has empowered her to act? Vision and purpose, the desire to serve, and the need to be obedient to Christ's commands are her empowerment.

One day maybe we will see Laverne's script played out on the big screen, or on television, or on video. I hope so. And we will know that behind Barbara's story of faith and sacrifice in Lebanon lies another story of faith and sacrifice in the suburbs of Nashville. Another lamb is roaring. Wolves beware.

✳

I am so thankful for all the lambs of God who roar at every level in the movie industry to help make Jesus known.

5

Lambs and Music:
Notable Sounds

One of the great serendipitous and totally unexpected blessings for me from the writing of *Roaring Lambs* has been the relationships engendered with people professionally involved in Christian music. For whatever reason, the artists, writers, and business executives involved in the Gospel Music Association have embraced the book and its message more totally and more enthusiastically than perhaps any other single group. As a result, I have gone to Nashville many times as well as to other places where Christian music people gather.

From being only an enthusiastic fan with great appreciation for a wide variety of Christian music, I have, amazingly to me, become close friends with many who are involved in the writing, performing, production, and distribution of the Gospel message through music. I have been afforded a fairly up close, in-depth look at the Christian music industry as well as at the individual careers and ministries of many of the people involved, which is not only fascinating but also encouraging.

Obviously, nothing as big and complex as the Christian music business is totally free of problems. And, with every successful effort to promote the Gospel, the Evil One attacks. Unfortunately, not all of his attacks are successfully repelled.

To begin to understand Christian music, it is important to understand that it is both an industry and a ministry. It is instructive to note that at the Christian music summit held annually at Estes Park, Colorado, there are two major speeches given. One is "The State of the Industry" given by John Styll, the articulate and highly respected publishing executive. The other is "The State of the Ministry" given by the Reverend Scotty Smith, who is the de facto pastor to those involved in Christian music.

The good news is that Styll thoroughly understands the ministry aspect of the business and Smith thoroughly understands the business aspect of the ministry. The problem is not that the two parts of the enterprise are completely antagonistic; rather it is the age-old struggle that Jesus spoke about—the difficulty of serving two masters. I have been impressed with the commitment that the leaders of Christian music have to the ministry side of the undertaking, while at the same time realizing that the ministry advances only as far as the business will take it. I have seen no tendency on the part of significant leaders to dilute the message, although there are, of course, different views on how it should be delivered. Certainly, the Gaither Vocal Band and the Maranatha Singers are musically very different from the Newsboys and D. C. Talk, but their messages about who Jesus is and why he came are essentially the same.

The most apparent angst in Christian music among the most thoughtful and prayerful of those involved is not about how to sell more records and more concert tickets. Those efforts do demand and receive much attention, but the real feelings of stress in the industry relate to who the audience is and who it should be. About 99.9 percent of Christian music is performed for Christians, which is certainly not all bad. The best of the music *should* bless, encourage, and inspire the body of Christ. It builds up those in the faith. But for those in the industry who take the command to be salt and light seriously, this is not enough. Nor is it enough for those who see the Great Commission as a mandate and not a suggestion. So, the struggle for Christians is about obedience to those commands; about how to take the music into the world and make it speak to, and sing for, those who do not know Christ; about how to use it to draw others to him; and about how to be roaring lambs—lambs among wolves.

The struggle is made significantly more difficult by the fact that most of the Christians who love Christian music are very jealous lovers. Most of those who sell Christian music at the retail level seem very strongly committed to keeping it for their regular Christian customers. As one Christian radio executive wryly put it, "Christian music fans are much more likely to forgive Michael English for his moral failure than they would be to forgive him for crossing over into mainstream secular music." Rather than being thrilled when one of the stars of Christian music succeeds with a wholesome record played on non-Christian radio, most Christian fans see this as selling out. Strange. Perhaps it is the Christian music *fans* who need to read *Roaring Lambs*.

With this as background, perhaps it is not too surprising that the two biggest stars in Christian music are also the two most persistent of the roaring lambs. They have the talent to take their music everywhere and enough support among their Christian fans to weather the criticism, of which there is plenty. I found out about the amount and character of this criticism when I wrote one rather innocuous paragraph about one of these stars, Amy Grant, in *Roaring Lambs*. I said:

> The best way to stop the spread of popular music with its vulgar suggestive lyrics is to record great music that uplifts the human spirit. Christian artist Amy Grant retards the spread of evil every time one of her records plays on a secular radio station. Those who criticize her for "crossing over" into the secular world with music that is not distinctly Christian forget one thing. Her music takes up the airtime that could have gone to one of the multitude of recordings offering only degradation and moral rot. Amy Grant is being salt in the world. She's high on my list of candidates for the Roaring Lambs Hall of Fame. One Amy Grant hit record provides more salt for a decaying world than a thousand sermons decrying the evils of popular music or nationwide boycotts of recording companies. We need more Amy Grants much

more than we need more reactionary sermons. We also need Christian musicians, talent managers, producers, and record company executives to bring real salt to the whole influential popular music industry.

That one paragraph produced far more vitriolic criticism than everything else in the book combined. It produced at least 95 percent of all the criticism directed at *Roaring Lambs*. And those who wanted to criticize me for praising her typically reached me by telephone at home! There were to be no impersonal letters to the publisher for them. They wanted to tell me in person how wrong I was to praise Amy Grant for crossing over and selling out.

All the criticism was worth it. It strengthened my belief that I was right. I still believe she is a Roaring Lambs Hall of Famer. And, I got to meet her.

Amy Grant

The first thing that struck me about Amy Grant as I sat down to join her, her husband Gary Chapman (also a talent and a person I admire), and two other mutual friends is how much more beautiful she is in person than when seen on television or from afar at concerts. She is certainly very telegenic, but even the best cameras and the best lighting cannot capture her radiant glow. The second thing that impacted me as we began to talk is her "presence." I had seen this in sports stars such as my friend Arthur Ashe. Amy Grant has presence in abundance.

We talked about my book, the paragraph in it about her, and the criticism it had engendered. I learned much about the criticism she receives personally and its impact on her. She told me about its beginning.

She does not recall which album started it. She is not quite sure which tour she was on. But she does recall that she was backstage getting ready for a concert in Detroit when it happened. "A bouquet of flowers came to my dressing room before a concert, and it had this long list of names signed to it. It was a petition of some kind. I mean it was long. It took a lot of effort to put together. I was just thrilled to have the flowers. And when I opened it up, it was basically a group of people saying, very judgmentally, that I'd obviously turned my back on Jesus and that I needed to get my heart right, and that they were all out in the audience. They basically thought I was going to hell in a handbasket. And I remember just crying my eyes out in the dressing room, thinking, 'People are so brave behind a pen. Nobody out there even knows me.'" Some Christian fans are pretty tough.

Being true to your artistic vision is not always easy—being salt, being a lamb among wolves, never is—but for Amy Grant it is a necessity. Since 1977, when Amy's first Christian album, *Amy Grant*, started people listening to her music, Amy's life has been lived under a microscope. Along the way, she has challenged many to enlarge their visions of Christians in culture. Eight of her albums have gone platinum, with several songs dancing all over the top of *Billboard* magazine's charts. Amy has gone places she never dreamed of going. She has visited Camp David to watch movies in a cabin with her husband and former President and Mrs. Bush. She has appeared on all the top morning television shows, several daytime talk shows, *Larry King Live*, and all the top night shows. She has sung on the Grammy Awards (and won a few to boot), has hosted her own nationally televised Christmas show, has sung an introduction for ABC's *Monday Night Football*, and more and more and more.

Along the way, there have been those in the church who have written her off as someone who had sold out. They stopped playing her music on their radio stations and listening to it in their cars or homes. But a great many caught her vision for making music that appeals to those beyond the Christian subculture, those out there among the wolves. And today, a whole new portion of the secular music industry is open to value-laden music, for which we can thank Amy for her willingness to be true to God's artistic vision in her own life.

Nancy Hatch, a marketing specialist with the Baptist bookstore chain, says in the *Bookstore Journal*: "Amy Grant allows you to capture an audience that might not (usually) come into a Christian store." Hatch says that Amy, in effect, has built a bridge with her music that has allowed people drawn to secular music to be introduced to Christian ideas, and more explicitly, to Christian singers. Knowledgeable salespeople can clue customers into what is going on with Amy Grant and think of other artists that they might enjoy listening to. The bridge she builds is a bridge of salt.

Yet, Amy admits that she has never sat down with the idea of writing a song that would "impact the world." She has never really had an agenda, she says, except to write music that is an honest expression of who she is. As someone committed to Christ, this commitment naturally finds expression in her work. But, she notes, it does not always have to come out in theological sounding words.

"I think that as a creative person, I do not have a big agenda when I sit down to write a song. For me, writing is the way I chronicle life or capture a feeling or freeze a moment in time. When it comes to deciding which of those songs should go on an album, I know that I am most affected by music that builds me up on the inside. So I'll make song choices in light of my experience with music, which is: 'I want this to be a positive experience.'"

It just so happens that in Amy's case, her music and her persona have an unusual appeal. Says one Top 40 deejay, Linda Silver of Washington, D.C., Amy has a "wonderful acceptance quotient with our listeners." That acceptance quotient is largely a function of Amy being Amy. And if she could offer one piece of advice to others interested in becoming cultural influences through art, it would be this: "I have never had a game plan [that, she says, she leaves to the giftedness of her management] ... but I am happy exercising my gifts. And I would just say, 'find contentment exercising your gifts.'"

To this day, Amy asserts that she could still be happy simply singing her songs at the Koinonia Coffee House, where she began. "I'm not downplaying the fact that I'm thankful for the success I've had. I mean it has radically affected my life and the lives of a lot of people that I know. But I think it [my happiness] stems from the fact that I'm just doing what God [created] me to do."

Does that sound simple? In one sense, it is. As a Christian and an artist, Amy wants to say that you do not need to do anything but be yourself, do your creative work, and trust God. "In the creative world, you know you birth a flame and you tend that fire and you feed it and breathe on it and nurture it and it's going to either stay the size it is, or go out, or grow," says Amy. She comments about many of her friends in the music industry: "I know people who are very talented, who have given their lives to Jesus and trusted him for every step, but their talent has never gone anywhere. And I think that you just have to be true to what you feel compelled to do on the inside, and trust that it is God speaking to you."

Has God given you a vision? Has he given you talent as an artist? Has this book inspired you to enlarge your vision to take salt into the culture, to be a lamb among wolves? Wonderful. But Amy makes a good point. It is your responsibility to catch a vision and then nurture your abilities according to that vision. Then, you have to leave it with God to do with it as he will. That can mean stretching yourself like you never imagined and taking risks some might think are crazy. It certainly meant that for Amy.

She recalls some of the reaction when the word got out that she was working on her first album targeted for the secular market. "When my musician friends closest to me found out that I was working on a pop album, I had several reactions. One from a really good friend was, 'If this fails, then you've gone from being a big fish in a small pond to possibly falling on your face, and, if you fail in a big pond, then it sheds a bad light on our industry.' That was one viewpoint. But once again, the way my creative side works is really more like saying, 'You know, I feel compelled to do this.' And I told this friend, 'Look, if I go down in flames, at least I was answering the voice in my own heart. If I try to start working off everybody else's agenda or reading somebody else's script, and then it fails, well, I've not only ... missed the boat, it wasn't even my boat. I'm sitting there trying to meet somebody else's expectations.'"

In the process, Amy has taken some lumps too. Working in a broader cultural context can be trying, and the answers are not always black and white. "This is kind of old hat, old history, but when I did decide to put out the album that had 'Baby Baby' on it, the record company came to me and they said, 'What we really want in the first video is to show you are a real person.' And they said that the hardest perception they fight is the Barbie and Ken perception of a Christian. They even said to me, 'We wish we could deliver this first single to the radio stations in a brown bag with no name on it, because it's a great song, but the untouchableness of the religious culture to people in mainstream music is a real turn-off.' So we really talked about doing a video for 'Baby Baby.' I thought that it would be real cute to do a bunch of babies in diapers, and I was bouncing that idea off one of my nephews who was in his teens and he said, 'That sounds like one of the worst ideas I've ever heard of.' I tried to put myself in his shoes and I thought, *You know, you're right. What people want to see is a spark. What they want to see is chemistry.*

"So I went and hired an actor, much to the shock and amazement of people who had known that Gary and I had been married for a long time. But I wanted somebody that was going to do a good job. I wanted somebody acting with me who was very comfortable in front of a camera. So I interviewed a lot of different guys with the help of a video company, and we just went in and worked hard. I felt that I wanted to express in this film a relationship that girls would see and go, 'Ah. I want to be in love like that.' And the same for guys too. Something fun and obviously filled with self-respect. And two people that are really interacting. It's not a sex sell. It's just a man and woman having a great time. I was down in the trenches, doing my work, going, 'Now, what would I want to see?' Well, I pop my head up out of the trenches and there's gunfire over my head," she laughs.

Many months after the video's release, the gunfire is still going off over her head. I was recently doing a radio talk show on a Christian station about the criticism I received for praising Amy Grant in *Roaring Lambs*, and the host's only comment was, "Well, she really crossed the line in the *Baby Baby* video."

For lambs among wolves, criticism goes with the territory. Charlie Peacock experienced the same kind of criticism when he wrote a song about love among married Christians. It is almost as if many Christians do not believe that the "ah" that Amy spoke about relative to "Baby Baby" is possible or legitimate for Christians. I am so thankful that it is. We need to be more creative and more mature in expressing and appreciating that "ah" emotion. We are not being fair and honest with the world or with ourselves when we are not able or willing to celebrate the "ah" that God allows in our lives.

To do what Amy has done, you cannot take yourself too seriously or think that you are God's only gift to music or art. Amy certainly has not. In fact, she knows that she has limitations, and she laughs at the times that they have come forth in living color—like one of her most embarrassing episodes ever, which she recounted in *Campus Life* magazine. "Probably the worst thing that ever happened to me musically was singing the national anthem at a 49ers/Raiders game. We were on a tour. And I'm pitiful with the national anthem. I just did it because a bunch of guys in the band wanted tickets to the game. As I stepped out to the middle of the field, I had earplugs in my ears, but could still hear, 'And now singing our national anthem. ...' Gary was yelling from the side, 'Pitch it low, pitch it low!' And I got out there and I got so nervous—it's a huge stadium there in San Francisco—I just started in, 'O, say can you see'—way too high. I was already in falsetto by the end of the first line. I could hear Gary screaming from the sidelines, 'Start it over!' But I couldn't. I couldn't start it over. When I finished, there was great applause. At the end it *sort* of resembled the national anthem. But I didn't really know what I was doing. I was petrified."

Since 1977, Amy Grant's life has become awfully complicated. Besides singing the national anthem in a stretched falsetto at a pro football game, she has a talented husband and their own three children to care for, everybody and their uncle wants an interview with her, and all around her there are the trappings of what being a successful artist in the broad culture offers—money, fame, meeting new people, going to interesting places, and on and on and on. This challenge may face some of you if you give everything to God. For some of you, God may bring amazing success, as he did with Amy Grant. You may find yourself encountering and experiencing the highs and lows, temptations and pleasures, that being famous brings. How would you handle it?

"On a deeper level," Amy told a *Nashville Banner* reporter in August of 1994, "it's hard for me to be in this culture and still hold onto the values that I have always believed in. So much of the world I live in whets my appetite for new things. The message I'm getting is that what I've got is not enough." It is the same message that the world sends to everyone, and it should encourage and strengthen you to know that it is sent to Amy Grant as well.

One of the best pieces of advice Amy ever got came from her former youth group leader and current comanager, Mike Blanton. He told her that "life is a process." That is good counsel. As we grow in our vision of what it means to be Christians in the arts and in culture, we need to realize that we are engaged in a process of becoming who God wants us to be. Amy feels that the becoming is much more important than setting out to impact others.

"I think that my calling is just to embrace today, to be most aware of the needs closest to me, and beyond that, of my friends. Gary's mom and dad have a cabin here on our farm and, you know, there are times that I look at my life and I am so overwhelmed that I want to laugh and cry. I mean, too much of a good thing is still too much. Years ago, my mother-in-law said, 'Amy ['cause she's very down-to-earth and has had an incredible impact on a lot of people— and she's never even been on a magazine cover], this is what I pray: God, today lead me to those I need and to those who need me, and let something that I do have some eternal significance.'

"That sounds so simple, but that's how I feel about my life. I mean, for all I know, tomorrow my singing career could be over, really. And I feel like having achieved a certain amount of what the world considers success, what I try to say to fellow artists is, 'Let's don't take the publicity side of this so seriously.' You know, there doesn't have to be any such thing as competition in music, because everything is so unique. And if the musicians are not having a certain amount of fun, then, really, what's the point? I mean, music is the uplifting element, even in Scripture."

With the success of her 1994 release, *House of Love*, Amy's music has continued to uplift millions of people. And she remains thrilled that her music actually serves as a conduit to introduce others to God and his love. In April 1994, Amy was honored with the *Pax Christi Award* from St. John's University in Minnesota. The award recognizes unusual expressions of Christian faith and values. Amy is only the third woman to receive it. In her acceptance speech, Amy told those gathered about a trip she had made to the shore with three nieces who had never seen the ocean. "We drove and parked in the parking lot on the opposite side of the highway. I said. 'Close your eyes. You're not going to believe this. Close your eyes.' My heart was pounding because I got to be the lucky one to make this introduction." The four climbed to the top of an old wooden bridge, and then Amy said, "Open your eyes.

"And they saw that water and started laughing and screaming, because you know what? The postcards don't do it justice. TV and surround-sound don't come close. The next thing I knew, those girls were running down the other side of those steps, straight into the water, with their dinner clothes on and everything." Amy continues: "I think the love of God is like the ocean. It's the greatest component of our world even though we don't see it a lot of the time. What an honor for me to get to introduce so many people to such a grand thing."

Amy Grant is a musical lamb among a lot of discordant wolves. She deserves our attention, support, gratitude, and prayers.

Michael W. Smith

If Amy Grant exudes a sort of regal beauty, Michael W. Smith emits good old charm. Something about "Smitty," as his friends call him, just says goodness, wholesomeness, and solidness. He is, of course, one of the greatest looking guys alive. *People Weekly* magazine has listed him among the "beautiful people." When my daughters, both very enthusiastic Smitty fans, learned that I had met him, that we had become friends, and that we were going to do a radio series together, they could hardly stand it. They christened us the "ultimate odd couple." The very dashing Tennessean coupled with the old tubby Texan just did not compute for them. Seeing photos of Smitty and me together causes them to just break up. It is all very humiliating. Yet Smitty is the least self-consciously handsome guy I have ever met and is seemingly oblivious to how he looks. In his recording studio in a Nashville suburb, he goes around unshaven and dressed "way down." Yet, the less he seems to care, the better he looks!

He may not seem to care too much about his appearance, but there are things in his life about which Smitty cares very deeply. He is so open, so up-front that you only have to be with him about five minutes to know what he cares about. He loves his family. He loves music. He loves the Lord Jesus. These loves take him to many places.

One such place is a glorified Louisiana juke joint just across the Texas border. A top-rated Texas radio station was throwing a party for its teen listeners in the neighboring state, where it is legal for eighteen-year-olds to drink beer. And drinking they were. Guzzling is probably more accurate. Michael peered through the murky dark at the rowdy rows of teens—about seven thousand of them, all under one roof. He sensed a larger demonic canopy of oppression hanging over the place. Along with mostly rhythm-and-blues musicians, Michael was there as a favor to the radio station, where his song "Place in This World" was number one on their playlist. It was 1992, and Michael was one of America's hottest new pop commodities. He placed his hands on the keys and began singing a soft tune called "Emily." As he played, a low chorus of boos filled the hall. The sound got bigger and grosser. Drunks were yelling and cursing at him. A full can of beer struck his shoulder. Michael, a strapping West Virginia boy, checked an urge to belt one obviously drunken guy sitting right below him. Things were out of hand, and Michael was getting a little afraid. He switched to an upbeat number. By the time he finished his set, everyone was cheering. Michael was just glad to get out of there. "I almost got killed," he recalls. "I was outnumbered." A lone lamb among many ravenous wolves.

Talk about getting beat up by the world. Michael experienced it—literally! Being a big-time contemporary musician and a committed Christian is not all Dove Awards and music video fantasies, at least not if you are in the business for the reasons Michael is. He is there because he loves to play music. He is a singer, composer, and entertainer. God created him for music; it is his joy and, gratefully, his job. Some people drive taxis—Michael writes songs, sings them, and rips up the keyboard. (In 1992, Michael was chosen one of America's top rock keyboardists by *Keyboard* magazine.) But because God has his heart, he also does his work, like any Christian should, for a higher reason. "I'm a minister," Michael says. "Whether you sing music or sell cars or work in a factory, you're a minister. I'm an entertainer. People come to hear me sing. That's what people do. They buy my records. But I also think that I have a platform where I can really affect a lot of people's hearts."

People certainly do come to hear him sing. I got a firsthand lesson of his drawing power. Shortly after I had met him and had begun to work on the radio series, Michael was scheduled to sing in Dallas, my hometown. His performance was to be a part of a big summer-long outdoor music festival featuring big-name artists. Smitty was scheduled to perform on Saturday, and the evening before, Willie Nelson had drawn ten thousand fans to the event. Now, in Texas, they do not come much bigger than Willie Nelson. Driving to Michael's concert with my family, I said, "This could be kind of embarrassing. Willie Nelson drew ten thousand last night. Michael may have a hard time matching that." How little I knew. Michael broke all the festival records when twenty-two thousand fans came to sing along with him on almost every song. He connected with that huge crowd in an almost magical way. It was a very special, inspirational evening. I will never worry about his drawing power again.

All this means that Michael sometimes ends up in an overblown teenage playpen singing a song of hope to rowdy, love-starved, drunk kids who show their appreciation with well-placed cans of beer. But Michael is not running. At least not until he has finished playing. "I'm not one to play it safe," he says. But it also means that this same guy, lauded in *People Weekly* magazine and the recipient of multiple Dove Awards, an American Music Award as "Favorite New Adult Contemporary Artist," and a Grammy, might end up spending a weekend at Camp David with the president of the United States and his wife.

Michael did just that a few years ago. He and the Bushes talked about music and foreign policy, among other things. They really hit it off. Then, culminating the visit, Michael performed a special concert for about one hundred select presidential friends in Camp David's chapel. There sat Michael in this quiet, quaint sanctuary, amidst the great leaders of the world. A hush softly cloaked the room. There were no beer cans this time! Michael set his fingers on the keyboard, and moved into one of his most-loved songs, "Friends." Out in the audience, tears welled up in the eyes of world leaders. Prime Minister John Major and his wife sat absorbed in the melodic words. So did the Bushes. Then the room filled with applause. Politicians and military brass were all clapping and smiling. Michael W. Smith was salt, a roaring lamb. "Who knows what happened in that chapel service?" Michael notes.

Who knows? And that is an important point. We are not called to keep score. We are just called to be obedient, to be salt and light. We may never know for sure whom God touched that day—or the day Michael played to the group of thankless Texas teens. But we can be sure of this. We would not even have cause to wonder if Michael had not been faithful in the late 1980s to the vision to perform his music for as many people as would listen. That is when Michael, following the lead of close friend Amy Grant, took his music beyond Christian stores and radio stations and out into the secular market. That is when he became a roaring lamb among wolves.

Today, Michael is out there in a land of lost souls that many Christians label as Babylon and declare off-limits to believers. On the televised 1993 Country Music Awards, he was slip-slamming his fingers all over the keyboards as part of an all-star country band in one blues segment of the show—Smitty, amidst the best the country music world had to offer. Did you notice him? Maybe not. It was not Michael in the round; it was not Michael playing on tour, as he did in 1994, when he pulled off one of the top-ten tour events of the secular music year, according to Pollstar's midyear report. This was just Michael doing what he loves, what God created him to do, and he is doing it among the kind of people he enjoys and at the top of his profession. At the same time, Michael was building new friendships with key music people. "To me, it's all based on relationships," he says. "I think that's how you lead people to Christ. All of a sudden, as a result of playing that gig at the CMA show, I have new friends—some Christian, some not. Maybe I can have an effect."

Believe me, Michael is not just blowing smoke here. He is absolutely one of the most down-to-earth, successful, talented people with a Southern drawl that you will ever meet. And he loves Jesus and seeks daily to serve him. Combine all that with "killer blue eyes, fluffy blonde hair, classic profile, and stubble" ("sometimes," as the *Milwaukee Sentinel* newspaper noted, "the impression is [singer] George Michael with good intentions"). What?! But the fact is, that about sums up the guy. And people sense that Michael is real and cares. Anyone who had been present, as I was recently, when one of his daughters was baptized and had seen the love and pride he exuded would know for sure how real he is and how much he cares about those in his life.

There was a time a few years ago, after Michael's song "I Will Be There for You" hit number one on the mainstream adult contemporary charts, when the soap opera *Another World* invited him to make a cameo appearance. It is one of several gigs that Michael has done that has raised the eyebrows of some fellow believers who say he has sold out. But, of course, they do not see Michael behind the scenes. While taping the show, Michael was able to meet most of the actors. At one point, he found it appropriate to give a CD to one guy, which opened a chance for him to talk about his faith. To be a lamb among the wolves, you must go where the wolves are.

Then there was the time that Michael hosted the VH–1 Top Twenty music video show. That, too, got some Christians mad. How could Michael appear on a show that was supported by Budweiser commercials? It really was not that hard. "Nobody knows that I got to share my faith with one of the executive producers of the show," he says. It happened as a result of Michael just being Michael. One producer just kept watching Michael as the taping went on. At one point, they talked a little about each other's families. She continued to notice how nice he was, how full of peace his life seemed, even when he had makeup artists scurrying around him flipping brushes in his face. What a contrast she saw between

Michael W. Smith and the normal infantile, egocentric, demanding, wired, and strung-out performers who are the norm in her life. Finally, during one break in the taping, she approached him. "What is it about you?" she asked. "You're different."

Am I wrong, or is that not the question most Christian manuals say represents the ultimate evangelistic coup? Michael, calmly and assuredly, responded with the right answer. "I hope it's my relationship with Christ," he told the sincerely baffled producer. Right there in the middle of taping, he took time to say, "There is just no way to explain to you the peace I have because of that relationship." Actually, he did not have to explain it. His life had just showed it to her. He had just given her a demonstration. Michael has a God-given peace about who he is and what he is doing.

Michael drew on this same peace when he, like friend Amy Grant, moved from explicit Christian into so-called secular music. In September 1991, the *Wall Street Journal* featured Michael in a front-page story about his and others' crossing over into the mainstream music market. "It is a crossover movement as tricky as it is potentially lucrative," the article said. The writer explained that people such as Michael have the "awkward job of staking out a middle ground between the sacred and profane." I don't know if this writer was a Christian or not, but she got it all wrong in the same way that far too many Christians continue to get it all wrong— thinking that God deals in two categories: sacred and profane. This just is not so. God created the whole world, including music. People came along, particularly Christians, and created categories, saying that only songs that explicitly mention God's name are sacred and all those that do not are profane. But just because a song does not mention God does not make it profane. And conversely, some can agree with conviction that some songs that *do* mention God are profane in their triteness and low level of creativity.

But the backlash occurred nonetheless. As Michael was rising to popular stardom with those outside the defined walls of contemporary

Christian music, some Christians questioned his motives. One well-intentioned teen told the *Journal*, "I worry that he will throw away his message and lose his ministry to make it in the secular market." Too few Christian music fans understand that one way Christian artists throw away their message is to continue to sing it only for believers who have heard it over and over and never take any salt or any light out into the darkness where the wolves are. Another person predicted that Michael would lose some of his Christian fans with his move into the mainstream. One Alabama radio station pulled Michael's and Amy's records after both appeared as hosts of VH–1. The station told the *Bookstore Journal*, "The artists will not return to our playlist until we are satisfied that a change of heart has taken place and their testimony is not one compromised by associations with secular rock, alcoholic beverages, and other destructive products," referring to the beer ads on the VH–1 network. (I wonder how this radio station handles the Gospels' accounts of Jesus' eating and drinking with publicans and sinners!)

Michael has always tried to steer clear of debate. He respects those who disagree with his career and ministry choices, but wishes they would not put him and others "in a box" by insisting that they have to perform only connect-the-dot lyrics in order to be both Christians and musicians. He wants excellence both lyrically and melodically. "I'm not going to try to make a record for the Christian or the pop market. Just let me be who I am." He is saying, in effect, that as a Christian, all he does should be done to advance God's kingdom. It does not matter who buys the records.

And people do buy his records. In 1991, his album *Go West Young Man* was released by Geffen Records. The lead song, "Place in This World," climbed to number six on *Billboard* magazine's Hot 100 list and broke the top five on the national adult contemporary charts. The corresponding video climbed to number two on VH–1. Michael performed to over a quarter of a million people and received his fifth Grammy nomination, after having won a Grammy in 1989. By August of the same year, *Go West Young Man* and Michael's prior release both went gold. On *Billboard's* year-end chart, Michael was listed among the top fifteen male pop single artists of the year and among the top twenty-five adult contemporary artists. In 1992, he won his American Music Award for "Place in This World."

In the fall of 1992, Michael released the album *Change Your World*, which was certified gold just three months later. The album's lead song, "I Will Be Here for You," became number one on adult contemporary charts. In 1993, Michael's "Change Your World" tour played to a half-million people, and the album neared platinum. All the while, Michael has remained dearly loved by the vast majority of his fans who make up the contemporary Christian market. In 1993, he was nominated for Dove Awards as Artist of the Year, Male Vocalist of the Year, and Contemporary Album of the Year. Readers of *CCM* (*Contemporary Christian Music*) magazine voted *Change Your World* Favorite Pop Album and Michael their Favorite Keyboardist. He tied for Favorite Pop Singer.

*

Maybe it is not so tricky to maneuver through the world of the profane and the world of the sacred at the same time. Being a lamb among wolves is not so much about being clever as it is about being obedient. It is not so much about being talented as it is about being faithful and about relying on God's protective and enabling power. It is a lot about being authentic the way Michael is. When he and Amy Grant sing songs with a positive message, sometimes even ones that mention Jesus as the answer, it registers in everyone's heart, whatever world they live in—be it a Louisiana juke joint or the White House. Perhaps their songs and concerts are like a trip through C. S. Lewis's Narnian wardrobe, taking all kinds of people to places their hearts long for, as well as teaching them lessons that God longs for them to learn. All the while, people are having fun, which is not a bad thing. Amy and Michael know that Christ waits like a gentle lion at the end of the adventure and at the end of all their songs. He is with his lambs, particularly and powerfully when they are out among the wolves.

6

Lambs and Sports:
Action-Packed Plays

In *Roaring Lambs*, I wrote, "More than in any other area of American life, Christians are providing salt in almost every activity involving sports." And since I continue to make my living in sports and sports television, I can report to you that I continue to feel that this is true. Sports, with all its problems, is still an area in which Christians and the Gospel are, by and large, respected and welcome. Even in sports, however, Christians are a decided minority. They are still lambs among wolves and must be vigilant and dedicated if they are to be productive for God's kingdom.

This chapter gives me the opportunity to stress once again one of the major emphases of this book. I want to be very sure that no one gets the idea that the only successful lambs among wolves are high-profile, high-visibility people. Certainly, we have included many of these kinds of lambs, but we have done so primarily as an encouragement to everyday rank-and-file Christians such as you and me. I want you to know that successful and respected athletes are out there on the front lines, but, even more than that, I want to be sure that you know that your front line, wherever it is, is just as important in God's sight. It is just as possible and *just as necessary* for the rest of us to be energized, active, obedient, and productive for the Lord Jesus as it is for any of the "stars." The battle for the hearts and minds of men and women goes on in all strata of society, and there is no hierarchy of importance. All are vital. We need the high-profile people in the opinion-setting areas of society to be faithful so as to better set the tone, to build a better climate for our every-day witness for Jesus.

So, as we think about lambs in sports, we want to consider some of those who have been faithful outside the headlines and away from the spotlight. For me not to consider these and not to laud them would be unthinkable and terribly ungracious. After all, because a faithful man saw the possibility of reaching boys for Christ through sports, I have the joy of knowing and serving Jesus. This man was not a sports star, was not trained in sports, had a full-time job out-side sports, but he put all his available time and energy into bring-ing boys into a saving relationship with Jesus through sports. Sports was never an end in itself. It was only a means to an end, and the end was always Jesus.

I was far from the only one this man was able to reach through sports and far from the most important. At one time three of his "boys" were teaching and coaching in Christian colleges. And one has gone on to become the president of one of the nation's out-standing Christian colleges. I had the great privilege and joy of pay-ing tribute to this man—my father in the faith—at his funeral cel-ebration. After ninety-two years of sterling service on earth, he exuberantly crossed heaven's home plate and was called safe. "Well done" echoed and reverberated around the celestial palaces.

So, it is important for all those involved in sports at *any* level to see their position as strategic and vital in the effort to build God's kingdom. Some may see those who coach church and Sun-day school teams as operating at the very lowest levels of sports. They may be the lowest levels as the world ranks sports, but they can be the major leagues as far as eternal consequences are con-cerned. The key for anyone is to consciously and deliberately plan so that being salt and light is the ultimate goal. Sports in church, Little League, high school, college, and the professional arena can all be fabulous ministries. So can all the ancillary activities that go along with sports.

Waddy Spoelstra

One of the greatest roaring lambs that I know of in sports was a sportswriter. Waddy Spoelstra was a hard-drinking, hard-living, typically crusty journalist until he met Jesus. He then became a non-drinking, family-loving, sweet-spirited journalist. He was a key "beat" man in Detroit, a town where sports are taken very seriously. Waddy was often among the wolves, especially as he covered the Detroit Tigers. He was often ridiculed and even suffered physical persecution for his beliefs, but he hung in there. He demonstrated love even to those who reviled him. And, not coincidentally, he was a superb newspaperman.

Now well into his eighties and living in Florida, Waddy devotes all his energies to serving the Lord. He is a spiritual mentor to many in professional sports. He publishes the *Christian Sports Insider*, which keeps Christian athletes and those who pray for them up-to-date on things important in their lives and is distributed free of charge to all who ask for it. Waddy also writes a regular column called "Waddy's World" for *Sports Spectrum*, the leading Christian sports magazine. Waddy Spoelstra was also one of the founders of the Baseball Chapel movement, which ministers to professional baseball players. He is a Roaring Lamb Hall of Famer.

Almost every sports fan has heard of Dave Dravecky, the brilliant left-handed national league pitcher who lost his arm to cancer and who now brings inspiration to many as he ministers through speaking and writing. He is a hero to millions and a very special hero to Christians. But how many Christians know Byron Ballard? Not nearly as many. How many know Bill Watts? Even fewer.

There is a Waddy Spoelstra—Bill Watts—Byron Ballard—Dave Dravecky chain that beautifully illustrates the rewards of faithfulness and the magnificence of God's plans when lambs really roar. Waddy Spoelstra founded Baseball Chapel. Bill Watts was the Baseball Chapel representative who was there the day minor league pitcher Byron Ballard's mother died, and who led Byron to Christ.

So, by the time Dave Dravecky was assigned to room with fellow pitcher Byron at Amarillo, Byron was able to patiently take Dave through the Scriptures and prove that Jesus is Lord. Wow! Waddy roars, Bill roars, Byron roars, Dave roars, and the crescendo builds and builds. Do you begin to see why every Christian is important and vital? Do you see why it is necessary for each one of us to take Christ's admonition to be salt and light very seriously and very personally? Remember, no matter where you are in sports, you are playing in the highest levels of the major leagues when you are playing to build God's kingdom.

Stan Smith

Have you ever played the game in which you are given the name of a person and you must immediately come up with a one-word description of that person—one word that captures the essence of who that person is? If I had to play that game with tennis great Stan Smith, the rather old-fashioned word *steadfast* would be my choice. There are many other words that can and have been used to describe Stan, but *steadfast* would be my word.

A disclaimer is in order here. On the one hand, Stan Smith has been a close and cherished friend for many years, so perhaps you should consider what I write about him with that in mind. On the other hand, Stan's life and career have been so closely followed and minutely documented that he is pretty much an open book. Certainly during the years when he was at or near the top of the tennis world, the cameras and the microphones were all pointed his way.

Stan's life is a great sports story. Told that he was too awkward and clumsy to be a ball boy for a Davis Cup match, he went on to become one of the most graceful, fluid, and powerful players of all time. He was steadfast in his effort to be the best.

In 1972 and 1973 he was the best, the officially ranked number-one player in the world. During those golden years, I had the privilege of seeing Stan up close and personal—on the courts, in the locker rooms, in the players' meetings, in the restaurants, and on the planes as the tennis tour moved around the world. Reigning at the very top of the sport, Stan was gracious, considerate, and friendly, even to the crowds of well-wishers, backslappers, hand shakers, and autograph seekers—the kind of flotsam and jetsam that always surround winners.

Sometime during the latter years of his incredible career at the top of the tennis world, Stan's shoulder began to fail him. He still played and still won regularly, but he never again dominated. He soon went through a period when he did not even win very regularly. Those who were close to him knew that pain accompanied every swing of Stan's racquet. But most fans had no idea that Stan's shoulder was so bad because he never complained, whined, or made excuses. Struggling with his game and the accompanying pain, Stan continued to be gracious, considerate, friendly, and helpful—steadfast.

The crowds were no longer as large. Most of the well-wishers of the winning years were off following a new champion. I even saw some of Stan's so-called friends and business associates, those who had been happy to capitalize on his success, become snide and mean-spirited in regard to Stan. Stan remained steadfast.

Stan's steadfastness presents another principle for lambs among wolves. Remember that while the world will always follow what it considers to be a winner, Christ is with us always. The world is with us win or tie. Jesus is with us when we cannot even suit up, when we cannot play at all. Roaring lambs know this and remain like Stan—steadfast.

Stan Smith's life and career were inextricably intertwined with Arthur Ashe's life and career. They were determined competitive rivals on the court and dedicated friends off the court. I once was present to hear Arthur pay one of the greatest tributes to Stan that one athlete has ever paid another. They were playing in the biggest match of that particular year, with millions of dollars on the line as well as the title World Champion of Tennis. It was an extremely close and thrilling match before thousands in a sold-out arena and millions watching on television. The match was eventually decided on one point.

With Stan fairly deep in his court, Arthur hit a well-disguised drop shot, a shot designed to barely clear the net and then bounce as low as possible, giving the other player almost no chance to reach it before it bounces a second time, ending the point. In this instance, Stan made a desperate lunge for the ball, stretching his 6'4" frame to the maximum. He just reached the ball and almost miraculously flicked it back over the net and past Arthur for a win! But wait a minute. Was the ball that Stan hit "up"? Or had it bounced twice before Stan's desperate lurch and scoop? Even the crowd in the stadium did not know. With replay after replay, even the television audience could not tell. The umpire, the man in the tall chair officiating the match, could not tell. Even Arthur, right there in the action, could not tell. Only one person on earth, Stan Smith, knew whether the ball was up or not when he had hit it back for that decisive point. As tennis rules dictate, the umpire asked Stan if the ball was up. Stan said it was. Arthur said nothing and went back and played the few remaining points in the match.

As you can imagine, the postmatch interviews focused on that crucial decisive point. On camera and before millions, Arthur was asked why he did not protest, argue, or ask that the point be replayed. Arthur's reply was a classic. "If Stan says it was up, it was up." Wow! What Arthur was saying was that even in the crucible, even with everything on the line, you could count on Stan Smith. What a testimony Stan had earned. He had earned it with Arthur over many years, while playing countless matches and traveling the world together. "If Stan says it was up, it was up." End of conversation.

As you seek to be a roaring lamb living among wolves, can those who watch your life say the equivalent about you? Another of Stan Smith's Davis Cup teammates said about him, "He has a great inner calm about him. I think he has the most integrity of any man in sports." If we really want to represent the Savior, that is the kind of reputation we will seek to earn.

All during his tennis career, Stan stood out from the crowd, not only due to his height, but also because of the amazing composure and grace with which he handled and still handles life on and off the court. He will tell you: "The very best way for a Christian in professional tennis to have a witness is, first of all, to conduct yourself on the court and react to circumstances that come up as a Christian."

For instance, there was that U.S. Open in 1971 when many players protested and bemoaned a ban that had been instituted on throwing racquets and using abusive language. In the midst of it all, *Time* magazine reported, "Stan went serenely on his way, demolishing everyone he met." Who would have thought that a Christian could have such a testimony by demolishing other players? But in this case, it is the finest example of a witness that I can imagine. While other players acted like children, embarrassing themselves and others because they could not curse and throw racquets when they did not get their way, Stan's inner peace, a function of his relationship with Jesus Christ, said to the tennis world and to the public at large: "You don't have to be like these folks! You can be like Jesus. And you can win at the same time!"

Another instance possibly shines even brighter for Americans and especially for believers. Stan recounts in his 1977 book, *It's More Than Just A Game*, that in 1972, when he was at the top of his game, the American Davis Cup team was able to travel, for the first time ever, to defend their title in communist Romania—the land of the now-infamous butcher, Nicolae Ceausescu. Ceausescu told the security agents who were guarding Stan and his teammates that "heads would roll" if the Americans were hurt, a possibility that proved to be very real for the Americans. The country was fanatical about its two bad-boy players, Nastase and Tiriac, both known to do or say just about anything to wrangle a point their way. In broken English, Nastase boasted that getting the Americans on the slow

Romanian clay courts would make "Godzilla [his derisive name for Stan] feel like he was serving on the beach." Amidst tight security and mocking fans, the Americans felt the danger.

But Stan had a new cohort in Christ, Davis Cup captain Dennis Ralston, himself a former hothead who had recently accepted Christ. The two prayed after arriving in Romania. They knew that the Romanians would go all-out to win the Davis Cup or steal it if they had to. More than that, they knew that the antics of Nastase and Tiriac and the taunting of the crowd would challenge their witness for Christ. About this time, Stan received a letter from his wife: "You are representing the U.S. and Christ, and it won't be as important for you to win the matches as it will be for you to represent the Lord well to all those people around the world who will be seeing the competition." Stan shared the letter with Ralston. They agreed: Representing Christ and America came first; saving the Cup came second.

Cup play began well. Stan opened in singles play by beating Nastase, that year's U.S. Open champion. But then Tiriac, trailing American Tom Gorman two sets to none, began resorting to ugly tactics. After a couple of calls did not go his way, Tiriac went berserk, using every four-letter word in the book against the umpire. Then he said he was quitting the match, surely a move to pressure the umpire amidst a hostile, partial crowd. "I'm not going to play," he told the neutral Australian referee. "Then I'm going to default you," the referee replied. "Default me and see what happens," Tiriac threatened. He slowly motioned to the stands filled with seven thousand angry Romanians. "Please, you've got to play, and I've go to do my job!" the referee pleaded. Finally Tiriac returned, but only to question yet another call. The linesman quit. The panicked referee begged him to stay, fearing he would have to call the match, which would be a certain death knell, figuratively if not literally as well. Then, out of nowhere, a replacement linesman appeared. They finished the match, and Tiriac's antics turned the match his way. He won, making the remaining Davis Cup picture look bleak for the Americans.

Stan and his doubles partner, however, managed to wrestle the third match away from Tiriac and Nastase—one of the best doubles teams ever—in straight sets. That left a final encounter: Stan against a crazed Tiriac, who was playing impassioned tennis in his final Davis Cup event in front of his rabid countrymen.

"I felt like I was competing against all of Tiriac's relatives, ancestors, and neighbors," Stan recalls. The two split opening sets. Then with Tiriac serving in the third, the Romanian began his antics. Worse than that, the referee had told Stan the night before that he would have to win the match big because he could not afford to rule against Tiriac on close calls. It was 30–love, and Tiriac served a shot that was long by at least a foot. But Stan, taking no chances, burned a baseline forehand back, which Tiriac hit into the net. "Out!" Stan heard the umpire's call, figuring he was simply hearing Tiriac's serve being called late. But instead, the umpire was calling Stan's return, which had landed well inside the baseline, long!

It was a point on which it would have been easy to break down. With thousands of screaming fans, and Tiriac delighting in the call, Stan turned to his fellow Christian and team captain, Ralston, who was sitting on the sidelines. Ralston, the former hothead, just gestured calmly, as if to say, "This is what we expected. Remember our goal." Stan finished the set and won 6–4, but Tiriac won the next set 6–2. Now the fans were yelling, "Teer-reee-ack, Teer-ree-ack!"

Stan closed his eyes and prayed, "Please, Lord, give me the strength to handle this situation." Then he began the last set with a service ace and won the set 6–0. Stan walked to the net to meet Tiriac. "I don't respect you as a person anymore," said Stan, as always consistent, honest, full of integrity, and steadfast. During that tense episode in Romania, the world saw a Christian who was not only up to the task skill-wise, but was able to glorify God in the midst of the most adverse circumstances.

It was in even more adverse circumstances that Stan's friend Arthur Ashe called on him for help. Because I was also one of the very few that Arthur told about his contracting AIDS from a blood transfusion, I know how much Stan and his wife Margie did for Arthur and his family during those terrible difficult days before his death. When Arthur told me the devastating news, he told me he was also going to tell Stan and was asking the two of us to pray for him and provide spiritual counsel. As always, Stan Smith was there for him. Arthur told me several times of his great appreciation for the way Stan and Margie had stood with him and his wife and had given so much of themselves.

Stan has found many other ways to serve, even in the midst of a very busy tennis and business career coupled with a very strong commitment to his family. For the past twenty years, Stan has spoken in at least one London church during almost every Wimbledon tournament. He was one of the founders of a ministry that put a full-time pastor on the tennis tour to minister to players and their wives and has provided much of the financial support for it. Christian camping has also been an area of service for Stan.

At forty-five, Stan is still modeling his winning, Christlike attitude, though his arena of influence has expanded far beyond the tennis court. Stan still plays senior tennis events, but he has also worked at the top levels of player development for the United States Tennis Association. Wisely, USTA leadership has wanted Stan's influence among its up-and-coming generation of players. He has traveled the country, spending his time scouting and encouraging young talents in their aspirations to be the best players they can be. As you can imagine, young men and women have always hung onto every word of advice from the great champion.

What do they associate most with Stan? The same thing everyone else does—truth and steadfastness. Recently, Stan was giving his own children some advice for life. "I was telling my kids the other night that some key words for success after having a real relationship with Christ are persistence and consistency. It [success] revolves around desire—the attitude of never giving up."

Top businessmen and women as well as key figures in sports see Stan live out these two words daily, especially when it comes to his family. Stan operates in an arena where spouses and children often take a backseat to the "famous" family member who jets across the world, landing business deals or producing or playing in major sports events. But Stan, from the very beginning, made a commitment that his work could never overrule his family life or his calling as a father and husband.

So, when Stan arrives at Wimbledon this year, top sports media and business figures—including those who use Stan's name for endorsing equipment—will see Stan's wife, Margie, and their four children: Ramsey, sixteen; Trevor, thirteen; Logan, eleven; and Austin, eight, walking right along with him. To his great credit, Stan acknowledges Margie's ability to home school the children and "keep it all together," which enables the family to travel together to places such as Paris, Tokyo, and London. Margie Smith is also a very special pal of mine and represents the best decision Stan ever made. Her spiritual maturity and her commitment to God's Word and its principles are reflected within her family. (The fact that she is also gorgeous does not hurt any either!)

Then there is the quiet positive effect that Stan's solid Christlike presence has among his associates, especially fellow tennis players. Stan notes: "Sometimes players will ask me about something they might have read or heard about my faith and my past tennis accomplishments. A parent will often do the same." I am glad that Stan Smith is out there, a rare lamb among the wolves, to answer those questions.

Frank Reich

As an old sports guy, it gives me a significant measure of joy that some of the all-time greatest, most thrilling examples of being a roaring lamb have occurred in sports. One of the most productive ways to be salt is by winning a hearing through the quality of our lives, and then, when we have the platform, to use it wisely and humbly, to tell who Jesus is and why he came. Here is a classic story, told with the help of an Athletes in Action brochure, from the annals of the roaring lambs:

Frank Reich warmed up his car on a cold Buffalo morning, getting ready to drive to Rich Stadium. It was January 3, 1993, and he was about to start his first NFL play-off game. His opponent: the Houston Oilers. While the windows of his car defrosted, he listened to a taped song—a song he had played over and over at least a hundred times that week. The song was "In Christ Alone," sung by Michael English, with lyrics by Shawn Craig and music by Dan Koch.

Frank sat and listened to the words and music, which had inspired him all week during practice. The ice melted from his windows. The song ended. Frank headed off to the stadium. When he got there he sat in his car, listening to the song over and over. Finally, he pulled some paper from his football playbook and wrote down the song's words. He sensed that God somehow wanted him to share the words with someone that day, maybe a teammate, a friend, or even a stranger. Right there, Frank promised that he would.

Then he headed off to the game. Little did Frank know that he would—that very day—quarterback the greatest comeback in the history of the National Football League. Down 35–3 midway into the third quarter, Frank led the Bills to an amazing 41–38 overtime victory over the Oilers before a massive play-off television audience.

When he returned to the locker room, people were yelling and hugging, going completely crazy. Suddenly the Bills' public relations man signaled his way. "C'mon, Frank," he said. "I've got to get you down to the press conference!" That is when it dawned on him: "The Holy Spirit just hit me," Frank says. He fumbled around and found that paper. He walked down the hall and into a room packed with media. Standing behind the podium, an awestruck nation waited to hear his comments about the victory. Frank stepped to the microphone to start the press conference and read these words:

In Christ alone will I glory
Though I could pride myself in battle won.
For I have been blessed beyond measure,
And by His strength alone I overcome.
Oh, I could stop and count successes,
Like diamonds in my hand.
But those trophies could not equal
to the grace by which I stand.
In Christ alone
I place my trust
And find my glory in the power of the cross.
In every victory let it be said of me,
My source of strength, my source of hope
is Christ alone.
In Christ alone will I glory,
for only by His grace, I am redeemed.
And only His tender mercy, could reach
beyond my weakness to my need.
Now I seek no greater honor than to know
Him more,
And to count my gains but losses, and to the
glory of my Lord.

Frank Reich, a backup Bill's quarterback who has taken countless blows from a rushing defensive end, who has sweated out training campus, who has competed for ten years at the highest levels of athletics—this same man, at a moment when so many others would have basked in the glory of making NFL history—said that he "counts his gains but losses, and to the glory of my Lord." And he said it on NBC before one of the year's largest television audiences. "Rooooooaaar!" Salt? A saline river flowed from Rich Stadium that day! What a testimony! What a classic roaring lamb!

It is important to emphasize that Frank had no idea that morning what was going to happen. No backup quarterback sets off in the morning to make NFL history and command the nation's attention. None of that mattered to him. Frank was simply going about the business of being a committed believer, a lamb among wolves, staying closely in touch with God in his personal life and asking God how he would use him in his workplace. God arranged all the rest! Are there any lessons there for you? There certainly are for me.

"Football is like a car to me," Frank explains. "It's a vehicle to use to take me to places that he wants me to go and to do what he wants me to do. And, at some point, like a car, my football career will depreciate and wear out."

Playing at football's highest levels has not always been a piece of cake for Frank. He admits that his first four years were a struggle. He did not show well during preseason games. And his fifth year started much like the others. People began to question aloud whether he was a suitable backup for Jim Kelly. Frank's faith in God, and in God's desire for him to play pro football, kept him going. In that season's sixth game, Kelly separated his shoulder and Frank got his first start, on *Monday Night Football* of all places, against the undefeated L.A. Rams. Frank prayed and gave the whole game to God.

For three-and-a-half quarters, he and the team stunk. Still, he had a strong sense of peace. The Bills' defense kept the game close, and, with a few minutes left, Frank drove the team down the field for a touchdown to give them the lead, 16–13. But the Rams scored on the very next play from scrimmage to take a 20–16 lead with less than two minutes to play. With ninety-four seconds left, the Bills had the ball and were facing sixty-five yards of field before the goal line. Seven plays later, Frank "hit" Andre Reed, another Christian, for the win. The score: Bills 23–Rams 20.

Frank knew God wanted him in pro football as a witness. He paid his dues, weathered the criticism, and trusted God. He always trusted. And in time, God used Frank. If Frank had given up early when it was hard, he would have missed the thrill, missed the joy of seeing God use him in the Rams win, and, more importantly, in the Oilers win.

But being a witness in the NFL is not all press conferences and national TV appearances. Frank allows God to use him regularly in less dramatic ways. Every Monday at noon Frank and about six other Bills gather in a condominium near their stadium. Sprawled on couches and chairs, away from football fans and frenzy, they put behind them the game of the day before—win or lose. They are there for other business—heavenly business. Each man has committed to pray for several other players. They have the whole team covered. "It's a tremendous privilege for us to be able to pray for our teammates and to gather in the Lord's name." After ten to fifteen minutes in prayer, Frank leads a study from a Christian book, followed by sharing.

When Frank and his fellow believers take to the field, it is not unusual to have regular exchanges among players about Jesus, especially during the long, hot, stressful days of training camp when players are fighting to make the team. Frank notes, "There are players really hoping to make the team and just searching for some peace." It is not uncommon for someone to run to Frank, who plainly exhibits this particular fruit of the Spirit, and bring up his spiritual life. For some, it may be a desperate grab for some foxhole faith, Frank notes, but others are sincere and hurting. That is when Frank—who has been "on the bubble" himself—explains, "My sense of self-worth doesn't come from how I perform on the field. It comes from knowing that I am loved by the God of the universe."

Frank says the two things he most often gets to talk to other players and other people about are finding peace through God and how serving God is a motivating force to do his very best. A commitment to excellence at the highest level of sports is what Frank has, and others see it. But there are others things they do not see—something that just God and Frank's two little daughters know about. That something is at the bottom of being a successful Christian, a lamb who helps the wolves and is not devoured by them in the media-drenched world of pro football. There are nights when Frank's daughters, five-year-old Lisa and two-year-old Avíry, lie together in bed, scared in their dark room upstairs. Frank walks to just outside their room, opens the door, and kneels by the hallway banister. Then he starts praying. It is a comforting sight to his daughters.

For Frank, this is often a time to talk to God about football, like just after that staggering record-breaking overtime win. After Frank roared, reciting the words to "In Christ Alone," people in the media started debating the question: Was God on the Bills' side and not the Oilers' side that day? Frank was troubled by the question that he had helped prompt. "Something wasn't right about it," Frank recalls. So one night, kneeling outside his daughters' room, he asked, "God, what do you think about football?" That is when God answered with this analogy: Frank loves both his girls equally. When they play a game, it does not matter to him which one wins or loses. It matters to him that they play fair and learn the lessons they need to from the game. Frank might even rig the game sometimes for the younger daughter to win. Frank realized then that God felt the same way about football. He was not as much interested in whether the Bills or Oilers won as he was in the personal growth of the people on each team.

It is that kind of perspective that has carried Frank toward being a successful Christian in pro football. In victories and losses—both on and off the field—Frank knows that God is at work. When other players eye him, hoping to catch him slipping, when they delight in picking out his slightest goof and calling him "Hypo Christian," Frank knows that God is still at work. When he gets mail criticizing him for speaking publicly about Christ, he knows God is working. When the child of a best friend and former University of Maryland roommate Boomer Esiason (former Cincinnati Bengals and now New York Jets quarterback) was born with cystic fibrosis, Frank flew to be at his friend's side. Few words were exchanged, but Frank knew God was still at work.

The story does not end there, however. Some weeks after the Bills' win over the Oilers, Frank played more than half of the Bills' Superbowl XXVII game, when the Bills got plastered by the Dallas Cowboys 52–17, one of the most lopsided Superbowl victories ever. Says Frank, "I was devastated. I couldn't understand how God would allow us to get beat like that, especially after the Houston miracle." The first two hours of his flight home were torture. Finally, he realized that he could not take it any longer. He had to find some peace. He reached for his tape player, put on the earphones, and turned up the song, "In Christ Alone." Suddenly, the words took on extra meaning, with an application far more important than any football game. "The message I was hearing was that we can experience victory in all our circumstances through Jesus Christ," he says. Lambs 100–Wolves 0.

※

I am so thankful for all the lambs of God who roar at every level of sports to help make Jesus known.

7

Lambs and Television:
Direct Broadcasts

Sometimes, perhaps not often, but sometimes, it is possible to know too much. When CBS was about to begin broadcasting *Christy*, I knew too much about it. I did not know too much about the story, but I knew too much about the effort to bring it to television. I am not normally an overly emotional person, but the emotional impact of *Christy* being aired was so intense that I could not bring myself to watch.

As a television executive and producer myself, I know how very difficult it is to get even the most mundane and banal program on the air, one that conforms to today's network standards and expectations. Those difficulties are multiplied many times over when you are dealing with a program that honors God, one that has a bias toward him, not against him. And yet this is what we are called to do if we are to be salt in the area of television, that medium that has so much impact on today's society. This is what Ken Wales, the producer of *Christy*, was called to do. In answering the call, he gave seventeen years of his life before the first episode aired. He is still fully engaged with *Christy*. He is a roaring lamb and, working as he does in television, he is a lamb among wolves.

Ken Wales

As the sun rises through a mountain mist, a layer of fog hangs just above the hardwood treetops. Ken is watching from the deck of his house, which overlooks Tennessee's Little River. He is reading Scripture and praying about the day ahead. *There are so many people*

139

around a television production who have their own agendas, he thinks. He prays for peace when dealing with them today. After awhile, dressed in his khakis and tennis shoes, Ken climbs into his rental car and drives toward the fictitious Cutter Gap, his heart's home. This is where he is living out his dream, one that he has now been able to share with many others through television. His car arrives on a grassy knoll at nine-hundred-feet elevation. A spectacular view of the Smoky Mountains looms in the distance. A wooden school-house-church is just over the way, tucked beautifully in among green pines. Ken found this site eight years ago, when his dream was still just that, only a dream. Now he climbs out of his car and hits the ground running. *Christy* is waiting.

When one understands that it took seventeen years to get to this point, "you begin to realize the fact that what I have here is God's miracle. I am simply a steward of it," says Ken. In the book *Christy*, Catherine Marshall told the story of how her mother left her comfortable Ashville, North Carolina, home and traveled to Cutter Gap in the Tennessee Appalachians to teach poor children at a Christian mission. It is a story of Christy's personal growth and influence among the mountain people, of her battling the elements, of her female strength, and of her remarkable faith in God.

Ken Wales' story of bringing the novel to the screen is almost equally as dramatic, and is what makes *Christy* such an emotional experience for me. This story illustrates a person's having a vision for impacting our culture for God and persevering through whatever difficulties the world might put in the way in order to see the vision realized. Unfortunately, there are not many Christians like Ken, thoroughly committed to excellence in television, who are willing to sacrifice so much of themselves to tell the world a story because it brings salt to a society desperately in need of it. One hour of *Christy* going into millions of American homes on CBS does more to be salt than all the negative actions of protesters and boycotters that are too often the only Christian response to television. If you want to be obedient and productive for God's kingdom in the area of television, do not get bogged down in negative activity, and do not waste your money to help finance it. Support good things. Support people like Ken Wales who are striving to bring godly alternatives to television. Ken's faith in God and in the story's message have never wavered.

The son of a devout minister, Ken, now fifty-seven, enjoyed a highly successful acting career after being discovered by veteran actor Glenn Ford at Ken's Santa Monica, California, high school. He was the boy next door in *Father Knows Best* and the young radio operator in *Torpedo Run*. He worked as the understudy to Hollywood's legendary director Blake Edwards on such well-known films as *The Great Race*, starring Jack Lemmon and Tony Curtis; *The Tamarind Seed*, starring Julie Andrews; and the *Revenge of the Pink Panther*, starring Peter Sellers. After working with Edwards for fifteen years, Ken went on to produce *Island in the Stream* with George C. Scott, the television series *Cagney and Lacey*, and his Emmy Award-winning TV miniseries of John Steinbeck's *East of Eden*.

As you can see, Ken was deeply involved in the Hollywood scene. And all this time, he also remained deeply involved in his church and in his faith in Jesus. Ken's life should help answer questions about the possibility of maintaining one's faith in worldly situations. Christ would not have called us to represent him in the world if he and the Holy Spirit would not be with us and keep us.

In 1969, early in Ken's acting career, while working at MGM on the movie *She Loves Me*, he noticed another MGM movie in production: *Christy*. Years before, another Catherine Marshall book, *A Man Called Peter*, had been a smashing movie success for Twentieth-Century Fox. Now MGM was hoping to score its own coup. But *Christy* was canceled during filming when MGM changed management. The property got buried in the studio's cellar, along with scores of other dead movies—hidden from the light of day and out of the memory of almost everyone.

In 1976, Ken was visiting Bel Air Presbyterian Church when he saw a poster advertising an upcoming speech by Catherine Marshall. *Whatever happened to Christy?* he thought. He called MGM about acquiring the rights to the movie version of the book; they would not sell. A movie studio rarely will sell a property, even if they are not doing anything with it. Instead, they use it as a tax write-off. But Ken did not let up. He called Marshall's editor in New York City. "She's really disappointed that it never made it to the screen. You should call her," her editor said. Ken hung up and rang Catherine Marshall, who answered on the first ring. "Suddenly there she was," he recalls, "my idol was on the phone."

"I want to tell you something," Catherine said. "This very morning my husband and I had been in prayer for an hour and a half on our knees about *Christy.*"

"A chill—a beautiful one—went right down my spine," recalls Ken. During their conversation Catherine added, "Ken, maybe God has a way." These words would stick with him.

In the ensuing years, Ken and Catherine often visited in person. Ken also spent time with Catherine's mother, Leonora Wood, about whom *Christy* was written. He discovered that his and Catherine's theologies and philosophies of life meshed wonderfully. But in 1983, while Ken was working on a movie called *The Prodigal* for Billy Graham, he got a call from Catherine's husband, Len LeSourd. "Catherine has passed away," he said. He invited Ken to the funeral in Washington's National Presbyterian Church.

"I just can't make it," Ken said, completely frustrated that his workload would keep him away. Catherine was dead, and *Christy* wasn't done. He was discouraged. Later, however, he knew he had to make the funeral. He caught a red-eye flight to Washington, then a taxi directly to the church. It was raining, and the service was about to begin.

Ken dashed inside, flicking water off his raincoat. A man who appeared to be an usher greeted him by name and invited him to sit with the family. Together they walked down the cavernous church's aisle while the others watched the latecomer take his seat. Then the service began. Ken looked up. There, seated directly in front of him, was Leonora. There was Christy. The minister began reading the words that Catherine had written for the occasion. They seemed to speak directly to her friend Ken, about never quitting and always striving to do one's best for Christ. As he listened, he kept looking at Christy. A fresh resolve filled him to see the production through. After the funeral, family and friends gathered in the foyer.

"Thank you for coming," LeSourd and others told Ken.

"And thank you so much for arranging to have the greeter welcome me and seat me with the family," Ken replied.

"Greeter?" family members replied. "What greeter? We didn't even think you were coming."

"Well, he spoke to me by name and invited me to come and sit with you," Ken insisted.

Suddenly everyone looked at each other. "An angel?" they asked.

"Absolutely," Ken now maintains. It was a defining moment, and one that helped inspire Ken not to give up. When we are obedient, God is with us. He makes things happen.

About two years later, a window of opportunity opened to bring *Christy* up from the MGM cellar. Ken visited a church and saw an old friend who was still with MGM. He called Ken the next day. "Are you still interested in *Christy*?" he asked. "I certainly am," Ken replied.

He explained that Ted Turner was buying MGM and might be willing to sell the film rights. So Ken mortgaged his house, drew on personal savings, and lined up investors to buy a year-to-year option on the movie rights.

But when the stock market crashed in 1987, his investors evaporated and his hopes of making *Christy* into a movie plunged again as well. Then, in 1991, CBS approached Ken. They were looking for a dramatic television series whose central character was a woman with strong moral convictions. Ken, however, just could not see *Christy* anywhere but on the big screen, with the Smoky Mountains in all their wide expanse as background to all the action. So CBS created the highly touted *Dr. Quinn, Medicine Woman*, and for a couple of years Ken just kicked himself.

Finally, in 1993, a good friend and former coproducer with Ken of *Cagney and Lacey*, Barney Rosenzweig, was meeting with Jeff Sagansky, president of CBS entertainment. They talked about the success of *Dr. Quinn, Medicine Woman*. Barney began pitching some other ideas to Sagansky, who finally interjected, "You know what I have always wanted to make? Did you ever hear of a book named *Christy*?" Did he? He knew the guy who owned its rights. Rosenzweig called up his old buddy Ken. It is time to give *Christy* a run, he told his friend.

Ken hung up the phone and thought, *Maybe God does have a way.* Catherine's words echoed in his head. *Maybe,* he thought, *God's way is through TV, not a movie.* Then Ken's wife, Susan, reminded him of a prayer of relinquishment that Catherine had penned and that he had memorized in part: "Our relinquishment must be the real thing because this giving up of self-will is the hardest thing we human beings are ever called on to do."

Ken told Rosenzweig that they should go for it. The rest, as they say, is history. *Christy,* the television series, was born. Its first seven episodes received high ratings and reviews. And as this book is being written, it was basking in the glow of appreciation. Its two-hour, 1994 Thanksgiving special received warm critical acclaim.

Ken says one of the chief ways he can testify for Christ is through his show's commitment to excellence. As a Christian committed to excellence, he cut no corners when it came to his cast. He hired British cinematographer Michael Fash, five-time Emmy Award-winning director Michael Rhodes, Emmy nominee Kelli Martin as Christy, along with veterans Tyne Daly, Richard Kiley, and Tess Harper.

The show's excellent production speaks for itself. And its message of commitment and sacrifice and personal faith in God comes through loud and clear. But *Christy* has also done something else. It has provided a way for Christians to become positively engaged in television. The series and its sponsors have gotten more letters and cards than any other TV show in CBS history. More than that, churches, Sunday school classes, and other Christian groups have organized to promote *Christy* viewership. Other Christians have worked to help publicize the series in their local media. Because of *Christy*, the lambs have roared. At one point, Ken had received more than 3,200 letters and 9,800 cards at his house alone. They tell of children who are inspired by the positive role models and of teens who have enrolled in college to prepare for a life of service.

No one ever promised that doing it right would be easy. We do know, however, that obedience always brings joy. "The stories focus on the goodness of life along with its difficult challenges," Ken notes. While many other filmmakers and television producers tend to highlight the more grotesque sides of life, someone is finally there to depict a higher, more beautiful standard. The basic question a producer must ask, according to Ken, is: "Do I want to celebrate the sewer or the peaks of the mountains?" Obviously, it goes without saying that God's kingdom needs many more producers who will give us mountaintop experiences. Ken shows us this is possible—not easy, but possible. And he has shown us that with God we can dramatically make a difference.

Ken and his wife Susan have other avenues for witness also. Among the most important is through their attitude around other staff. They very consciously and deliberately try to exhibit Christlike character even in the often-trying and pressure-packed location shooting. "I just don't blow up. I try to find God's purpose and will in whatever the dilemmas are," Ken says. And others notice. "They come to us with their problems and their dilemmas. We share our hearts with them." This is called integrating Christ into all of life.

Too, I don't think anyone can watch *Christy* and not see a Christian's love for God's creation jump out at you. The mountains and valleys of the Smokies are breathtaking artistry. "Having a sense of being in God's world, and an openness to God's world, enables me to use to the best of my abilities, the gifting God has given me."

This has also meant that not only does Ken refuse to take the low road when it comes to recruiting staff and hiring equipment and artistic help, but it also means that Ken still pours his own money into the project, which has yet to produce a cent of profit to him personally, although everyone else definitely gets paid. "Whatever it takes, do it," Ken constantly tells himself. If the show makes it for four years and into syndication, then Ken might retire his personal financial investment. If not, there is treasure in heaven.

Sadly, Ken says that *Christy*'s message could have been even more profoundly Christian if its backing had come from Christian financiers, where he initially looked. But few could catch the vision. "Christian businessmen make you jump through a lot of hoops," he says. "Each denomination wants to make their vision of 'Becky Goes to Bible Camp.'"

Can we learn from this? Yes, we can learn the lessons that both *Christy* and Ken Wales have to teach us. In the meantime, who is willing to commit to a vision for great Christ-based work in the culture through TV? Are you willing to try to be a Ken Wales? Can you see the finger of God at work in Ken's life to bring *Christy* to millions? This same kind of hand is there to help mold and shape *your* culture-salting visions. Will you have a vision—your own personal version of *Christy*? It may be based solely in your neighborhood or rooted in your city. God does not expect us all to be involved in network television; he *does* expect us all to be salt. Your mission of saltiness may be occupational or merely as a part-time tithe of your time. But if you will be obedient, you too can know the joy of seeing the sun rise on your mountaintop, with your very own version of *Christy* waiting for your company. Go for it. Do it for Jesus' sake.

Ken Wales and *Christy* may be the most dramatic current story of lambs among wolves in television, but thankfully God has other lambs out there who are also being salt in this important medium. Since writing *Roaring Lambs*, I have learned of so many of God's choice servants who are laboring in these fields that I have been amazed and blessed. It is encouraging to realize that God is often at work in ways and in places outside our view. Obviously, there are never enough people, and we need to always be looking for ways to add to their number, but God is still sovereign. He still reigns. He has his people.

Michael Warren

Another person who is salting television with a witness for God is Michael Warren. Michael and his longtime partner, William Bickley, met at a small Baptist church in Beverly Hills. (Small Baptist church and Beverly Hills is not an oxymoron. The very fact that there is a small Baptist church in Beverly Hills where Christians meet and worship should be an encouragement to us all!) At the time of their meeting, Bickley was producing *The Partridge Family* and Warren was a producer at World Wide Films, Billy Graham's California-based film company. Warren was looking to expand his creative opportunities and his witness. Bickley suggested that Warren interview for an opening at *The Partridge Family*. Since then, the two have also produced and written for *Happy Days*, *The Love Boat*, and *Perfect Strangers*, to name just a few TV series. Currently they rule Friday night television, producing three Friday night ABC sitcoms—*Family Matters* and *Step by Step*, which they created, and *Hangin' with Mr. Cooper*, which they inherited.

What is the working philosophy for all their success? The bottom line, says Warren, is that "people are more important than programs." What is the foundation for this? One thing: Warren's Christian faith.

"We have become known for making a happy place for people to work," says Warren. That is one of two main ways in which he feels he can best represent Christ through his high position in television. The second mode of witness Warren concentrates on in his TV world involves the messages of the shows themselves. He and Bickley get a chance to be appropriately proactive in inserting messages with good values into their shows, and, conversely, they act as gatekeepers as well. "A lot of times it is sort of steering a show away from where you don't want it to go."

A case that illustrates both points occurred recently when Warren and his team decided to address the problem of sexual promiscuity among teenagers. They wrote a script dealing with the issue for *Step by Step* in which a character named Cody revealed that he made a moral decision to remain a virgin until he married.

Every week network officials sit in a conference room while each show's actors read aloud through the script. It is a chance for them, and the actors, to offer their critique to the writers and producers. After hearing this particular script, a network representative said, "Let's make this a safe-sex show."

"There are a million of those shows out there," Warren replied. But a show that honors abstinence, he noted, would be a fresh message. The show ran with its message preserved and received more positive mail than any episode Warren recalls ever being associated with in his television career. There was no negative mail.

Warren and Bickley then decided to do a similar show on *Family Matters*, which aired prior to *Step by Step*. Again, people wrote expressing appreciation for this rarely seen message.

Being this kind of salt is not new for Warren. *Happy Days*, because it was a period piece, allowed him and his partner to explore all sorts of family issues. Even Fonzi, the show's lovable rebel, proved to be searching for solid values and relationships that truly last, and he eventually moved in with the Cunninghams.

Warren jokes that he and Bickley became the show's "obligatory Christians," which meant that if the rest of the production team wanted a show with, say, a nun in it, their knee-jerk reaction was to call on this twosome. "We don't know anything about nuns!" they would crack. But they had managed to gain a positive reputation—no doubt due in part to their wonderful attitudes toward life as Christians in the network television workplace. Their input was therefore valued and sought after.

However, putting yourself and your Christian values on the line does not always produce laurels and standing ovations. Sometimes not even all their Christian viewers have appreciated Warren and Bickley's work. For instance, a couple named Frank and Carol on *Step by Step* are frisky and obviously have a wonderful offscreen sex life. "It's okay for a mom and a dad to have an active sex life," is the message Michael wanted to come across, but it has taken heat from some Christians. As we said earlier, that kind of opposition comes with the territory.

And sometimes Warren's efforts have backfired in other ways as his shows have explored Christian themes. For instance, as they developed the main *Family Matters* character of Steve Urkel—a socially rude but lovable and good-hearted goof—the writers thought it might make sense to explore his personal faith life. So they actually wrote a show in which Urkel proclaims that he has been born-again. The script, however, was tough to pull off with the actors, who had trouble understanding its central theme. Warren learned a lesson: "There is a limit to what you can ask actors to portray if they don't particularly understand the message." And if someone becomes born-again, then it would make sense that in ensuing shows their lifestyle and environment would reflect that. But that has not been possible to portray in the show, especially since the last thing Warren wants the show to be is preachy—a careful, thoughtful line he must walk every day. And yet, in some ways, Warren and

Bickley have crossed or blurred all the lines. They have done so by
just being there—by being lambs among wolves.

Ultimately, Warren says, it always comes back to relationships.
"People are not going to look as much at your TV shows as they are
at you. They are going to ask: 'Are *you* for real?'" "Like the guy recently
whose wife had just been diagnosed with a deadly cancer. He was
searching for his moorings as he faced losing his wife. He seemed to
be searching for an answer to the question, "What do you do when
things happen and tragedy comes into your life?" At one point Warren was able to share his personal convictions with the man. "You've
got to have something in your life that's eternal and lasting," he told
him. The man learned more fully of Warren's relationship with Jesus.

In Hollywood, as Warren notes, every kind of bizarre and unusual religion and philosophy is practiced. In a strange way, this
actually *opens* opportunities for talking with people about Jesus
because "the milieu of Hollywood is that nothing shocks it. So, the
reaction you get most often is, 'Hey, that's kind of interesting.'"

When I have spoken around the country and advocated that
Christians target television and the movies as careers of choice for
themselves and their children, some have reacted with concern. "Is
it really possible for my son or daughter to be in the entertainment
business and maintain his or her faith? Can they find any fellowship,
any support?" are their basic questions. Again, no one promised that
it would be easy. Whatever our occupations, we must be vigilant,
keep in close contact with Jesus, and rely on the Holy Spirit for
strength and sustenance. I hope it will help you to know that every
week on the Warner Brothers campus, a group of Christian actors,
writers, technicians, and producers gather to talk and pray. "'Keep
us safe from our foibles,' is one prayer that often goes up," Warren
notes with levity. "This is a job where there is a great deal of self-
induced stress," he notes. Warren himself supervises three shows and
240 employees. "My attitude is: 'It's just a TV show. I want to do a
great job. But it's just a TV show.'" Michael Warren's bottom line is:

"I think a person can make a difference," he says. "You come to work every day and ask God, 'What can I do to be responsible and treat people ethically and guide a script to where it will be wholesome?' It is a battle where you win some and lose some." That is the life of lambs among wolves.

Brian Bird

Another lamb on the television scene is Brian Bird. Brian is an almost prototypical example of a roaring lamb and has much to teach us all. Early on, he recognized that he had writing talent, so he did what almost every committed Christian does, he put his talent to work for the Lord in a Christian ministry. There is nothing wrong with that; every Christian ministry needs talent. However, Jesus also asks us to be salt. That means that some of us, more than just a few of us, must take our talent and put it to work for him adding salt to the world around us. Brian Bird is one of those people.

Profoundly influenced by Franky Schaeffer's sometimes criticized book *Addicted to Mediocrity*, Brian realized that he needed to be one of those working in the secular context. Others also fanned Brian's desire to serve. A godly uncle, himself a leading worship leader, was another person the Lord used to influence Brian. "This is an instrument you have from God," he said of Brian's writing skills. "Hone this gift. Play this instrument to God's glory." This positive involvement by a relative is one of the main reasons that I relate Brian's story. Too often moms and dads, aunts and uncles, and other relatives are obstacles to be overcome, rather than being encouragers to Christian youngsters who seek to use their talents to serve God in secular enterprises. The same relatives who often respond with praise and support when a youngster announces a call to the pastorate or other traditional ministry respond with fear and discouragement when a young person sees a way to use God-given talent to serve in a secular context. Pastors, too, are often shortsighted in these situations, citing the dangers of worldliness rather than the marvelous opportunities to be on the front lines for Jesus, relying fully on his saving and keeping power.

Brian was serving with World Vision when he began to understand the necessity of taking his writing skills out into the secular mainstream. I am afraid that most ministry leaders, when confronted with an employee's desire to use his or her talents elsewhere, especially in an area such as network television, react with horror and discouragement. To their everlasting credit, Brian Bird's bosses at World Vision not only did not respond that way, they saw God's kingdom in a broader sense, one that went beyond even their great worldwide ministry. Not only did they encourage Brian, they worked out a way to help support him while he further honed his talents and established himself as a network television writer. Always an admirer of World Vision, Brian's story deepens the respect I have for them. Their example is one for every ministry to consider.

Soon after leaving World Vision, Brian formed a writing partnership with fellow Christian John Wierick. Their breakthrough piece was a script telling the amazing story of a fourteen-year-old black child named Emmett Till whose 1955 lynching helped launch the modern civil rights movement. After that came assignments to write several sitcom episodes and TV movies. They were hired to adapt the South African stage play *Bopha!* into a movie. It was released nationally in the fall of 1993 starring Danny Glover and directed by Morgan Freeman.

Today, Brian Bird spends his days "feeding the beast," filling the relentless demand for scripts that goes along with being part of a successful sitcom. Brian has made it to the center of network television, and now he gets an opportunity to mold a segment of American culture based on his love for the Lord.

Brian made several stops along the way to his TV success, including a long stint in the Christian writing world, the very arena where many of you may now find yourself. Some of you may be reading this as students. Brian has been there too, wondering where and how to use his talent for God. He will even tell you that he was basically a *B* student all the way through school. He has made his way to the top by maximizing the talent God gave him and by a willingness to press on to do what it takes—with excellence. Still, Brian is so down-to-earth that he sees himself as a very normal Christian young man.

Are you inspired by Brian Bird's story? It started with a vision, was encouraged by an uncle who told him to use his gifts for God, and was strongly supported by the visionary leaders at World Vision who provided key help and encouragement. Today, Brian's story continues to play out in Burbank, California, among actors and producers, preparing a show watched by millions weekly. Perhaps the best way to describe Brian's faithful response is step-by-step—coincidentally also the title of the weekly hit on which he works with none other than Michael Warren.

＊

Are you inspired by the stories of Ken Wales, Michael Warren, and Brian Bird—God's lambs among the wolves of television? I hope you are. I hope you also realize that God uses many other lambs in many other, often less glamorous, ways in television, both nationally and locally. While all of us may not be called to produce or write for highly acclaimed network programs, all of us *are* called to be obedient to Christ's call for us to be salt in the world. Until he comes again, we will all be lambs among wolves. We need to be sure that we are faithful.

Epilogue

This book does not have an ending. It can't, because there is no end to the number of individuals who are living out the Gospel in the rough-and-tumble world of business, the arts, journalism, entertainment, professional sports—the real world. I hope it has been somewhat comforting for you to learn that our faith is being winsomely represented by some of the best and brightest in these influential fields. But I hope you have also been challenged to examine your own role as a roaring lamb.

For every Ken Wales struggling to create great television, we need hundreds of "ordinary" lambs who will roar in their own communities. Maybe it means using your business contacts to develop a relationship with the leadership of your local network affiliate. Maybe it means using your own creativity to produce a feature program for your local cable access channel. For too long, we've let "the other guys" control and influence television. Could *you* join Ken's mission to infuse television with material that honors Christ?

Maybe you aren't a business leader or you don't think you have the talent to produce good television. You realize that you may never write an article for the *Atlantic Monthly* or anchor the CBS *Evening News*. You tend to use the word "just" to describe yourself: just a housewife, just a schoolteacher, just a salesman. How can "just" an ordinary guy or girl like me become a roaring lamb?

You can begin by dropping the word "just." Jim Russell was "just" a small businessman until he caught a vision for seeing the Bible quoted in the mainstream press. Once he caught that vision, he was no longer just a small businessman—he became a tool that God used to place the Bible's powerful messages in front of millions of readers. If you think you will never really make a difference, you probably won't.

You also can find your voice as a roaring lamb by becoming more involved in your own community. Start right where you are. Attend school board meetings and offer positive alternatives when questionable policies and practices are proposed. Fight abortion by volunteering to serve as a crisis pregnancy counselor rather than picketing a clinic. Write positive, encouraging letters to civic authorities when they do something right. Attend wholesome movies and make a practice of thanking the theater manager for adding such films to the marquee. Support a local Christian artist by buying her paintings or sculptures. Coach a Little League team and teach impressionable young people about good sportsmanship, positive habits, and wholesome values.

Being a roaring lamb is really just putting the best face on your faith so that others see Christians as an asset rather than a liability. It means going back into the arena, rubbing shoulders with nonbelievers, and giving something back to a world that desparately needs it. It means focusing more on what you are for rather than what you are against.

It means clearing your throat, practicing a few bars, and then roaring the Good News with gusto in ways that draw others to the life-giving music of the Gospel.

I'll be listening!

Also from Bob Briner:

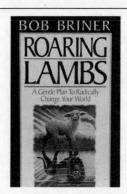

Roaring Lambs

*A Gentle Plan to Radically
Change Your World*

Do Christians belong in our culture?

Bob Briner thinks they do. And in *Roaring Lambs*, he shows how we can return to the "culture-shaping arenas" with the gospel. Christians can be the movers and shakers of social change—"roaring lambs" who infiltrate and impact their workplace and world with their faith.

Briner writes from his own experience as an Emmy Award-winning television producer. In *Roaring Lambs*, he takes you into the workworld to meet busy Christians who "roar" on their jobs. You'll find culture-shaping strategies anyone can use. And there's also a discussion guide to help you and your friends take your faith from heartfelt conviction to hands-on action. Now you can learn to roar with conviction—and change your world.

What others are saying about *Roaring Lambs* . . .

. . . bound to arrest the attention of the thoughtless Christian, and the thoughtful non-Christian.
William F. Buckley, Jr.

Roaring Lambs *is one of the most convicting and challenging books I have ever read.*
Dave Dravecky, author of *When You Can't Come Back*

Too often, the message of Christianity today is promulgated by "professional" Christians, smugly preaching to the converted. More difficult and more noteworthy—even more Christian—is what Bob Briner advocates: that what matters is to carry the Word and its goodness into the skeptical, multicultural real world.
Frank Deford, contributing editor, *Newsweek*

Squeeze Play

Practical Insights for Men
Caught between Work & Home

Caught in the struggle of balancing business, family, and faith?

Bob Briner understands what it means to be a man of God in the world of business. He knows the struggles and temptations. The loneliness. The ethical problems, sexual lures, and family concerns.

Briner also knows how to apply the Word of God to meet those challenges. His extensive experience in the worlds of professional sports and television production offers numerous case studies. From a personal invitation to attend the Shah of Iran's lavishly financed world class tennis tournament, to the ins and outs of sports television broadcasting, Briner demonstrates sound scriptural wisdom applied to life on the go. *Squeeze Play* brings Christianity to your daily battlefields.

What others are saying about *Squeeze Play*

I recommend *Squeeze Play* to Christians who are grappling with complex business and ethical decisions. The practical insights given to readers in all stations of life willl assist in each one's Christian walk.

Alvah H. Chapman, Jr., retired chairman and CEO, Knight-Ridder, Inc.

If you were moved by *Roaring Lambs*, as I was, you must give *Squeeze Play* a read. Briner is back—and his new book is better than ever.

Barry Landis, vice president, Warner Alliance/Warner Bros. Records

Bob Briner's practical tips on maintaining one's spiritual edge will help every Christian "squeezed" by the demands of his business or profession.

Franklin W. Graham, III, president, Samaritan e, Inc.